' her first book, Kryss Shane created an invaluable resource to help .nools become LGBTQ affirming environments. This time she is using her almost 30 years of experience and insight to transform workplaces. Although suicide is the second leading cause of death among youth, the highest suicide rate in the USA is among working-aged adults 45–60. One step towards reducing adult suicide is creating a workplace that affirms LBTQ employees and parents of LGBTQ youth. While the June 2020 Supreme Court decision protecting LGBTQ workers under the Civil Rights Act of 1964 was necessary, it was not sufficient to ensure workplaces were ming environments. Shane's book meets this need and fills this gap."

Jonathan Singer, *President of the American Association of Suicidology*

' s get down to business: whether you are a current business leader, eone dreaming or planning to become a leader in your industry, an ocate, or a customer who supports businesses invested in LGBT+ nsion, Kryss Shane consistently delivers as the most engaging go-to ch and educator on best practices for creating supportive and productive B T+ inclusive businesses and workplaces. Kryss' coaching and interactive essons, guidelines, and leadership challenges exploring how and why ating LGBT+ inclusive work life is good business practice presented here ld not be timelier or more on the money."

Andrea Shorter, *Co-Founder, Bayard Rustin LGBTQ Coalition; Former Director of Community Relations, Out & Equal Workplace Advocates; Former Director, Marriage Equality and Coalitions Strategies, Equality California; Inclusive and Safe Community Building Consultant and Strategist*

Creating an LGBT+ Inclusive Workplace

Setting out best practices and professional guidance for creating LGBT+ inclusive workplaces, this approachable and easy to follow book guides current and future leaders of all industries toward appropriate and proven ways to create safer working environments, update company policies, enhance continuing education and training, and better support LGBT+ people in the workplace.

Featuring real-life situations and scenarios, a glossary, and further resources, *Creating an LGBT+ Inclusive Workplace* enables professionals in all aspects of professional roles to integrate foundational concepts into their everyday interactions with staff at all levels as well as within the community to create an overall workplace culture that nurtures a welcoming, inclusive, and affirming environment for all. This book includes postcards from PostSecret as its foreword and more than a dozen exclusive interviews from the world's top leaders in a variety of industries with world-renowned reputations.

Enabling professionals in a variety of business roles to create an overall workplace culture that nurtures a welcoming, inclusive, and affirming environment for all, this book is an essential resource for independent readers, department teams, and entire corporations.

Kryss Shane, MS, MSW, LSW, LMSW (she/her) has been named by The New York Times and many national and international platforms as America's go-to Leading LGBT Expert. She has 25+ years of experience guiding the world's top leaders in business, education, and community via individual, small group, and full-staff trainings. She is known for making each organization's specific Diversity and Inclusion needs become more manageable, approachable, and actionable.

Creating an LGBT+ Inclusive Workplace

The Practical Resource Guide for Business Leaders

Kryss Shane MS, MSW, LSW, LMSW (she/her)

Routledge
Taylor & Francis Group

NEW YORK AND LONDON

First published 2021
by Routledge
52 Vanderbilt Avenue, New York, NY 10017

and by Routledge
2 Park Square, Milton Park, Abingdon, Oxon OX14 4RN

Routledge is an imprint of the Taylor & Francis Group, an informa business

Library of Congress Cataloging-in-Publication Data
Names: Shane, Kryss, author.
Title: Creating an LGBT+ inclusive workplace : the practical resource guide for business leaders / Kryss Shane.
Description: New York, NY : Routledge, 2021. | Includes bibliographical references and index.
Identifiers: LCCN 2020053601 (print) | LCCN 2020053602 (ebook) | ISBN 9780367699291 (hbk) | ISBN 9780367678128 (pbk) | ISBN 9781003143888 (ebk)
Subjects: LCSH: Sexual minorities–Employment. | Diversity in the workplace. | Personnel management.
Classification: LCC HF5549.5.S47 S53 2021 (print) | LCC HF5549.5.S47 (ebook) | DDC 658.30086/6–dc23
LC record available at https://lccn.loc.gov/2020053601
LC ebook record available at https://lccn.loc.gov/20200536

ISBN: 9780367699291 (hbk)
ISBN: 9780367678128 (pbk)
ISBN: 9781003143888 (ebk)

Typeset in Sabon
by Taylor & Francis Books

Contents

About the Author   x
Acknowledgements   xii
How Big of a Problem Is This?   xiv
Preface   xvi
Foreword by PostSecret   xix
Introduction   xxx

Section I — The Foundation: Terminology and Insights   1

    Section summary 1
    Safety 2
    Allyship 6
        Why It Matters That You Are an LGBT+ Ally 6
        Who Am I and What Traits Do I Bring to Allyship? 7
        How to Be an Active Ally 9
    Privilege 14
    Intersectionality 16
    Battle Fatigue 18
    Terminology 20
        In Broad Terms 21
        Sexual Orientations 22
        Gender Identity 26
        Additional Useful Terminology 35
    Coming Out 36
    Questions and Answers 39
    Research Your Resources 40
        Safety and Medical Emergencies on Business Grounds 40
        Health and Wellness Concerns at Home 40
        Safety Emergencies Occurring at Home 42
    In Closing 43

Section II — Scenarios: Test Your Knowledge   45

Section summary 45
Scenario 1 46
Scenario 2 51
Scenario 3 55
Scenario 4 59
Scenario 5 64
Scenario 6 70
Scenario 7 73
Scenario 8 77
Scenario 9 81
Scenario 10 84
Scenario 11 88
Scenario 12 91
Scenario 13 94
Scenario 14 97

Section III — Put Your Knowledge into Practice   101

Section summary 101
Assessing Your Workplace 102
 First Impressions 103
  Hiring Processes 103
  After Being Hired 105
 The Written Rules 107
 Introduction into the Workimg Environment 109
 Assessing Your Business 110
In the Office and Collaborative Spaces 111
Leadership and Learning Materials 112
How to Implement Change 113
Sample Scripts 115
In the Meantime/On Your Own 116
 Physical Space 117
 Inclusive Curricula and Printed Training Materials 119
In Closing 120

Appendix I: Opposition   123

 Business District Leaders (including C-suite and
 Board Members) 124

Business Leaders (including Supervisors and
Department Heads) 125
Company Employees 126
Employees' Families (including Spouses/Partners,
Children, and Other Loved Ones) 128

Appendix II: Interviews   129

Lau Viggo Albjerg, GlaxoSmithKline and
Colgate-Palmolive 130
Lauren Banyar Reich, LBR PR 134
Bill Barretta, The Muppets 137
Greg DeShields, Philadelphia Convention and Visitors
Bureau 140
Richard Gray, Greater Fort Lauderdale Convention &
Visitors Bureau 142
Sally Hogshead, How to Fascinate 148
Kenny Johnson, Philadelphia Phillies 152
Shelly McNamara, Proctor & Gamble 154
Brian McNaught, Corporate Trainer 156
Jerrie Merritt, Bank of Nevada 160
Gary Murakami, MGM Resorts International 164
Alfredo Pedroza, Wells Fargo 168
Howard Ross, Cook Ross 172
Josh Scott, GracePointe Church 177
Andrea Shorter, Inclusion Strategist 180

Appendix III: Additional Resources   185

Archives and Collections 186
Arts, Literature, and Culture 186
E-journals and Online Newspapers 187
Gender Identity and Sexual Orientation 187
General Resources 187
History 188
Legal 189
Organizations 190
Religion 191

Index   192

About the Author

Named by *The New York Times* and many national and international platforms as the go- to Leading LGBT Expert, both in America and throughout the world, Kryss Shane, MS, MSW, LSW, LMSW (she/her) has over 25 years of experience guiding the world's top leaders in business, education, and community via individual, small group, and full-staff trainings. She is known for making each organization's specific Diversity and Inclusion needs become more manageable, approachable, and actionable in financially realistic ways. This includes physical spaces, hiring practices, policies/procedures, and more.

Kryss earned her Bachelor of Science degree at The Ohio State University in the field of Human Development and Family Sciences, her first Master's degree in the field of Social Work at Barry University, and her second

Master's degree in the field of Education, specializing in Curriculum and Instruction at Western Governor's University. She has completed numerous additional training specific to teaching at the collegiate level, specializing in online education from Columbia University. She is currently working on a doctorate in Leadership at University of the Cumberlands, where she continues to focus on how to best educate people about LGBT+ inclusion and affirmation. Kryss holds social work licenses in the states of Ohio and New York, as well as numerous certifications in topics including providing online-specific education, mental healthcare and LGBT+ youth, suicide prevention, and many, many more.

She travels the world working as a consultant, educator, and corporate trainer, as well as appearing at events and conferences as a keynote speaker, an author, and a writer, all of which focus on making schools, businesses, and community leaders more LGBT+ inclusive. In addition, she is currently a teaching associate, lecturer, and liaison at Columbia University and an adjunct professor at Brandman University.

Throughout her career, Kryss has aided in the introduction of Gay Straight Alliances in numerous high schools, participated in the National Equality March in Washington, D.C., rallied for non-discrimination laws in numerous states, and has held or actively participated in meetings with numerous legislators to educate and encourage their participation in the Equality Movement. She has worked in concert with numerous equality-based organizations in a variety of roles to support, affirm, and celebrate the LGBT+ community. It is believed that Kryss is the first person to get a rainbow pride flag included in a country music video; an image of her in front of a rainbow flag and wearing a Harvey Milk t-shirt while participating in the 2009 National Equality March was included in the 2019 lyric video for Trisha Yearwood's "Every Girl in This Town."

Kryss is well-versed in the areas of sexual and gender minorities, including historical and current research. She has significant experience working with transgender youth, transgender military servicemembers, LGBT+ people struggling with suicidality, and others. This provides the foundation she uses to educate and guide professionals to better understand, accept, and communicate about and alongside the LGBT+ community. She continues to actively advocate for LGBT+ rights on the local, state, federal, and international levels.

In addition to being known for her work in the LGBT+ field, she is almost equally known for her lifelong love of tie dye (making her easy to spot in a crowd or at an event) and her never-ending adoration of NYC pizza.

Kryss is available to create curriculum around this book, as well as to teach this course at universities worldwide. Please contact her at ThisIsKryss.com to discuss your needs.

For additional consulting, speaking, or training requests and for interviews, please visit ThisIsKryss.com.

Acknowledgements

Much like becoming a business leader, writing a book does not happen without significant guidance, assistance, and support by others.

Thank you to my Chosen Family, individuals who have consistently chosen to prioritize our relationship, no matter the miles, no matter the circumstances, making me feel seen, heard, validated, and loved (alphabetically by first name): Bryant Horowitz, Dan Coleman, Deb Unger, Gail Vaz-Oxlade, Isaac Arrieta, James Monroe Iglehart, Janet Sasso, Jason Topel, Jeremy Mathis, Jessica Hardt Horowitz, Kara McElvenny Crowley, Karen Uslin, Kathryn Mathis, Kurt Broz, Lauren Banyar Reich, Lee Watkins, Melvin Abston, Mika Kaneshiro, Rachel Porcellio, Richard E. Waits, Toby Rogers, and Tyler Merritt.

To my Phillies: Jeanette, Cheryl, Debbie, Lois, Sandra, Michelle, and Stacey—thank you for being so authentically yourselves while being so willing to come together regularly to talk about everything and nothing. Thank you for trusting me with your stories and your lives and gifting me your friendship and your support.

Thank you to Saba, who loves me unconditionally. It makes me braver.

Thank you to Russ Lottig and to Christine Lottig for giving me perspective as I write and as I grow. While our lack of agreement is sometimes frustrating, it is invaluable, and it makes me better.

Thank you to business owners Susan Mankita (Sweet Grindstone) and Les Oppenheim (Special Events Catering by Les), whose varied ways of running their companies gave me insights both through observing their experiences and through watching their successes. Thank you to their son Benjamin Oppenheim who has been kind enough to share his parents with me.

Thank you to Jason Uveges and Troy Diana, incredible men who gave me unconditional support, who were gone far too soon, and who left me with a better sense of self and a stronger sense of purpose both professionally and personally. Thank you to John Lottig, the loss of whom kept me from remaining lost.

Thank you to Andrea Shorter; we met sailing through a hurricane, so perhaps it only makes sense that you have somehow managed to always calm the waters and point me in the right direction. I am forever grateful that I get the privilege of not only marching alongside you in our shared work but that I also get the honor of having you as my friend.

Thank you to Meredith Norwich, Julia Pollacco, Dominic Corti, and the rest of the incredible team at Routledge for their work and guidance throughout the publication, marketing, and success of this book.

Thank you to Frank Warren (my favorite fellow non-canine secret-keeper) for his contribution that created the Foreword and to the interviewees, each of whom are Rockstar industry leaders, kind and generous enough to share their experiences and brilliance with us all for the interview section within this book. The final product and the final reading experience are significantly richer and more soulful because of each of you.

Thank you to Marsha P. Johnson and Sylvia Rivera, John Lewis, and Justice Ruth Bader Ginsburg who spent their lives leading others and overcoming the odds whilst changing the landscape of America through their unending brilliance, tenacity, and grit.

In summary, this book is the culmination of everything I've learned about leaders and leadership, and everything I believe will make this world a better place. Thank you to those who take the time to read it, who make an effort to internalize the information contained within it, and who make consistent, persistent efforts to support and affirm LGBT+ community.

How Big of a Problem Is This?

Too often, people fear trying to start a conversation or intervene against negativity. This is not because they do not care or because they do not see the value in improving career and knowledge; it is because they fear saying or doing the wrong thing. However, doing and saying nothing implies agreement or consent with anti-LGBT+ behaviors and policies.

The Human Rights Campaign Foundation 2018 survey *"A Workplace Divided: Understanding the Climate for LGBTQ Workers Nationwide"* found that:

- Forty-six percent of LGBTQ workers say they are closeted at work, compared to 50 percent in HRC's groundbreaking 2008 Degrees of Equality report.
- One in five LGBTQ workers report having been told or had coworkers imply that they should dress in a more feminine or masculine manner.
- Fifty-three percent of LGBTQ workers report hearing jokes about lesbian or gay people at least once in a while.
- Thirty-one percent of LGBTQ workers say they have felt unhappy or depressed at work.
- And the top reason LGBTQ workers don't report negative comments they hear about LGBTQ people to a supervisor or human resources? They don't think anything would be done about it—and they don't want to hurt their relationships with coworkers.

A 2019 study by Out & Equal Workplace Advocates *"Workplace Equality Study"* found that:

- 78% of transgender people felt more comfortable at work after their transition and believe their workplace performance improved.
- 89% say they are very likely or somewhat likely to work for a business that does not discriminate based on sexual orientation or gender identity, along with other nationally protected groups.

- 68% of people say they are likely to shop at or support businesses that take a public stance in support of LGBT+ equality.

Now that we see the impact of what happens when silence prevails, it is clear that speaking up is necessary to protect LGBT+ people in business settings. As for knowing what to do, this book will guide you through the process so that you will feel confident in ascertaining problematic situations and policies, knowing who to speak with to make corrections, and knowing how to speak up in support of LGBT+ safety, security, and inclusion in your business setting.

Preface

This book was not created to push a political agenda, to turn current businesses or corporations on their heads, or to undermine professional experiences currently being provided throughout America. Instead, this book aims to enlighten the reader and encourage them to consider the ways that small additions or changes to existing offices and business practices may further benefit their employees professionally, socially, and emotionally.

Your personal beliefs about the lesbian, gay, bisexual, and transgender (LGBT+) community are your own. While I cannot guarantee you won't reconsider them by the time you've completed this book, please know that it is not my goal to focus on those beliefs. In your personal lives, it is, of course, your prerogative to make choices that best align with your personal beliefs. However, this book focuses on choices, behaviors, and actions taken within the professional environment while in the role as a leader.

Some question whether the idea of gay employees is new. It can seem as if people are constantly inventing new words to identify their sexuality and gender, making it easy to wonder if this is just some silly way that some adolescents are attempting to make themselves seem more exciting and unique. It stands to reason then that these attempts should not lead to any alterations within the workplace. Some believe that even acknowledging any of these terms only feeds a person's desire to create new terms and new words to stand out more and more from their peers. Others question why there seem to be so many transgender people all of a sudden. Many talk about how no one identified as such in past decades or in previous generations. In both situations, the answer is twofold. There were not many opportunities for people to live as openly as they do now when it is becoming safer in many states and many countries to publicly identify as something other than a society's typical expected identity options.

In addition, technology has also played a part. In past generations, one person may have felt a certain way and thought they were the only one in the whole world with those thoughts and feelings. Now, because of social media, there are additional opportunities for people to publish and self-publish their experiences, and because people are more easily able to connect to those they identify with, that one person no longer feels they are the only one in the world. Instead, they can hop on a computer or use a browser on their smartphone to connect with others in other communities across the globe who are just like them. Often, this experience allows for a significant amount of validation for the individual who previously thought they were all alone and that the lack of peers sharing this experience meant that their feelings must be wrong, and this indicated that something must be wrong with them. This resulted in many around the world feeling lonely, lost, broken, and unworthy. It is easy to see how a person with this belief could experience depression and why so many attempted or died by[1] suicide.

As the saying goes, there's safety in numbers. This is true with sexual and gender minorities as well. Now, support groups and friendship groups exist on social media, which bring people together from all over the world who would never have otherwise met but among whom shared feelings and identities exist. Simultaneously, video-sharing platforms allow individuals to document their life experiences and personal journeys, which can bring comfort in better understanding to viewers, regardless of whether they feel validated within their own communities, businesses, and families.

This book is not about whether there are gay people, whether transgender people are a "real thing," or whether there should or should not be dozens of terms people use to self-identify their place in the world. The reality is that there are gay people, there are transgender people, and there are people who self-identify using terms that may be unfamiliar to others. This then leads us to consider whether adults should acknowledge these differences, especially if the adult may believe an employee or colleague is using a word or term solely for attention. Some may even question how anyone should be expected or required to acknowledge these proclaimed differences, as they may remember that not long-ago mental health diagnostic manuals considered homosexuality and transgender identity to be mental illnesses. However, every major mental health organization has spoken out in support and acceptance of LGBT+ people for decades, using research and science to buttress their position that sexual orientation and gender identity are a healthy part of who a person is, not a mental health issue that requires fixing.

Now that we've established that LGBT+ people exist and that none of the science-based professional medical and mental health organizations identify these identities as mental illnesses, it is incumbent upon business leaders to recognize how business staff and business leaders impact their employees. Whatever your opinions, whatever your beliefs, it is likely universal that everyone who dedicates their career to the lives of employees wants those employees to be safe and successful. This is the basis of this book. By recognizing ways that LGBT+ employees feel unsafe, unwanted, and unworthy of acceptance, business leaders have the opportunity to work to minimize those experiences, to maximize the situations as learning experiences, and to help society create employees who have healthy self-esteem, an awareness and compassion for their peers, and staff with excitement for the future that they only get to see and experience if they are guided safely throughout their careers.

Note

1 The use of the word "committed" in the phrase "committed suicide" leads to connecting the act with a choice to perpetrate a crime rather than being the result of mental health struggle. As a result, the use of "committed" can cause many loved ones of those who died by suicide feel shame about how their loved one died, furthering their trauma and grief. In addition, using this word furthers mental healthcare stigma, which can cause people experiencing suicidal ideations or thoughts from seeking out support or help and thus being at higher risk of their own suicide attempt or death by suicide.

Foreword by PostSecret

PostSecret is an ongoing community mail art project. In the 15 years since Frank Warren created PostSecret, he has received more than one million secrets, mailed to him from all over the globe. The PostSecret website is the most popular ad-free website in the world, having had approximately 900 million views to date. Thousands of secrets have been on tour at museums throughout the world, including at America's Smithsonian Museum.

This project has become such a phenomenon largely because of the ways in which one person's secret has been found to be the secret of many. As such, to see the secret of one is to have the opportunity to identify that this one secret speaks for countless others who hold that same secret or that same experience inside of their hearts.

The following secrets have been graciously contributed to this book by Frank Warren, as he continues to support the mental health, suicide prevention, and acceptance of all people through PostSecret, a goal this book shares with the entire PostSecret community of contributors.

I wonder what they'd do if they knew their Fellowship of Christian
Athletes President is gay.
Because I am.

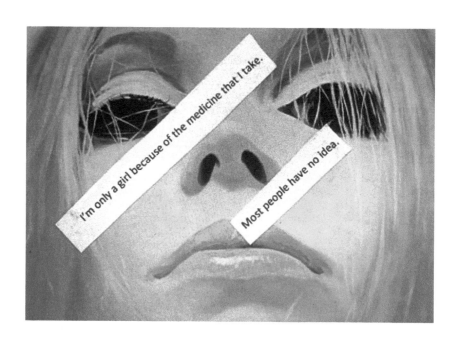

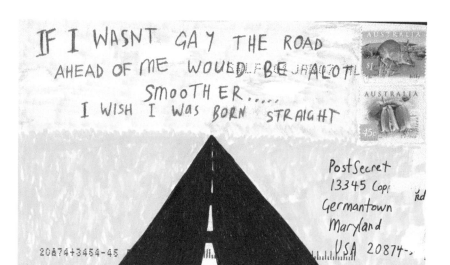

IF I WASNT GAY THE ROAD
AHEAD OF ME WOULD BE A LOT
SMOOTHER.....
I WISH I WAS BORN STRAIGHT

PostSecret
13345 Cop?
Germantown
Maryland
USA 20874-.

I am planning to kill myself
    at work.

I don't want any of the
few people who care about
me to find my body.

I know there's no chance
of that where I work.

PANTONE®
485

My coworkers said how upset they'd be if one of us COMMITTED SUICIDE because they couldn't imagine missing all the signs.

GUYS! I'M RIGHT HERE! YOU'RE MISSING THEM ALL!!

When I put a Pride sticker on my car, I parked in the back lot for two weeks, fearing a backlash since I wasn't out at work. I've been parking right out front for a month now, and nobody has said a word...

I would rather
risk spending my
life being called
"too politically
correct" than risk
spending my life
wondering if I could
have done more
to prevent someone's
suicide.

PEOPLE LOVING PEOPLE:
THAT'S THE ENEMY OF EVERYTHING
THAT'S EVIL.

Introduction

Before we began this book, let's take a minute to get really real. One of the biggest questions I find most people ask themselves before attending a conference, listening to a speech, or spending time reading a book is *Who cares?* For this reason, I will focus this book only on topics when there is a clear answer, not just to *Who cares?* but also to *Why should I care?*

This isn't because I believe you are incapable of making these connections yourselves, but because I recognize that, by the sheer nature of being a leader, each reader is likely to be focused on many aspects of their professional industry and trying to master them all. In many situations, books that are written for people of a profession are written by people who have never worked within that profession. This results in an entire textbook, reference material, or mandated required reading that works well in theory, but which professionals are swift to acknowledge could never work in practice.

This is why this book will be laid out to make it most accessible for you to find the information you need when you need it.

Section I offers foundational knowledge, including terminology and frequently asked questions. This will provide all readers with the opportunity to gain or review information, ensuring that they are up to date in current best practices regarding language and research.

Section II provides scenarios that allow readers to try out what they learned in Section I. Scenarios offer opportunities to think through various real-life business situations. Each scenario is followed by questions to answer as well as guidance so that the readers' answers can be deconstructed, to highlight best practices and to gain further insight into the best ways to meet the needs of the employee or business situation within the scenario. This section can be utilized individually, in small groups, or as a collective. This is a great way to test yourself privately, to collaborate within leadership teams, or to bring a leader-training seminar together to turn theory into practice!

Section III turns the hypothetical scenarios into real-life action! This section will guide readers in assessing their own business settings, provide scripts to reach out to supervisors to request to discuss making changes in areas where improvements have been identified, and to make alterations within one's own control. This provides the opportunity to discover where your business is successful, gives insights into how to work with your supervisors to make your business more LGBT+ inclusive, and offers methods to improve your own office, office, or workplace setting.

The goal of this book is not to make a reader become an expert in this field, but rather to provide foundational knowledge that encompasses the immediate needs of the LGBT+ people within your business, in a way that causes as little disruption to offices and businesses as possible. Also, ideas within this book are intentionally set to require little to no preparation time, and little to no expense to purchase supplies or materials. While a reader is certainly welcome to expand any of the suggestions provided or to outsource them by spending money or reallocating staff focus, or incorporating additional supplies and materials, it is not required.

It is my hope that the information you will read will allow you not just to find implementation opportunities within what you are already leading, but also that it will help you to understand that the nuances and ways of being mindful of the LGBT+ community can cause benefits to employees, staff, family, and the community overall.

Section I — The Foundation: Terminology and Insights

Section summary

In this section, you will find foundational information related to the lesbian, gay, bisexual, and transgender communities, as well as to other communities that are under the "sexual orientation and gender identity" umbrella. This includes considerations of safety, allyship, terminology, and frequently asked questions.

How to use this section

This section can be utilized individually or collectively. If you are reading this on your own, consider your current knowledge base and assumptions before each section, then read on and compare your thoughts with the information provided. This will allow you to spend as much or as little time in this section as necessary based on the insight you already have, correcting your misperceptions and filling in knowledge gaps as you read. If you are reading this in a small group setting, please encourage individuals to take time to think independently, then for the groups to share their thoughts with one another. After, the answers from the book can be provided, allowing all participants to compare their thoughts and the group's discussion with the correct answers. If the group is large, breakout groups can be assigned to go through this process in a more manageable way, thus allowing everyone the opportunity to share their thoughts and assumptions as they work through the information in this section.

Section take-away

The purpose of this section is to inform the reader, to correct misunderstandings and outdated knowledge, and to prepare the reader with the foundation necessary to best utilize the entirety of this book.

Safety

Until June 2020, there were no mandates of federal protection and this lack of requirements has too often resulted in no legal consideration for the lesbian, gay, bisexual, transgender (LGBT+) community at all. That meant that each state (and sometimes each city within a state) got to decide whether a person can be discriminated against for being LGBT+. What considerations and protections to provide LGBT+ members of a business community were also left up to specific cities or individual business districts or even individual businesses. With the newness of this, it means that there are likely to be many debates, lawsuits, and possibilities of legal loopholes. It also means that many in positions of power may not be aware of the new laws or they may be ill equipped to behave appropriately when they no longer have the option to avoid working with LGBT+ people. This can create situations where different businesses in the same community may have vastly different rules, policies, and procedures regarding the LGBT+ community. This information is vital to understand so that business leaders can be mindful of the life experiences of the LGBT+ people with whom they regularly interact.

In some places, there are legal questions and attempts to pass bills to undermine the success of LGBT+ people. These are seen with transgender bathroom bills, where it is legal to fire someone for being gay (or because someone just thinks a person is gay), and in situations where a city or state has a clear legal inability to alter a person's gender marker on their identification paperwork. In other areas, specific cities, business districts, or businesses may have created their own policies to ensure safety and inclusion of support in the business experience. When looking into LGBT+ people's protections or lack thereof specific to your own community, it is essential to consider not just what has happened within your business or business district, but also what is happening in the surrounding communities.

In some businesses, there are signs or stickers identifying a business or office as a "safe space." This program has been around for quite some time. The thought behind this, and its goal, is to identify which places and people do not allow homophobic, biphobic, or transphobic language or attacks. When coming out and being out were much rarer, it made sense for the goal to be rooted in recognizing where somebody would not have to hear horrible slurs. In more recent times, however, this is not enough. Now, the most inclusive and welcoming identification is that of being a brave space: a brave-space office, or a brave-space company.

This may simply seem to be a change in semantics, but it is not. In a safe space, there is a designation that homophobic, biphobic, and transphobic language and actions are strictly forbidden. In a brave space, it goes beyond this. Experts have realized that while it is crucial to stop horrible things from being said, it is insufficient to stop there. In a safe space, a homophobic statement is responded to by telling the employee that this is not acceptable and ending that type of talk. In a brave-space setting, the conversation is much different. Instead of shutting the conversation down, those in brave spaces encourage further discussion about what has been said or done. Rather than saying that it is not acceptable to use a word or phrase, it is asked why the person chose to use that word or phrase. The focus is not on shutting down the communication; it is on nurturing the communication so as to better understand the perspective of that person, and to encourage them to think through where their thoughts and ideas originate. Whether these are biased or bigoted, and no matter how overarching these ideas and ideals are, starting the conversation where that person is at allows the speaker an opportunity to recognize the impact of their words, to consider where their assumptions began, and to make sure that what they have said is what they genuinely feel and intend when they are using this type of language.

In a business setting, this may be somewhat tricky, because it is not always possible for a leader to stop an entire meeting or conference to talk through this process with one employee. It makes sense then that a safe-space protocol is used, as it is much more efficient to tell an employee to be quiet than it would be to sit with them and talk through why they said what they did. However, these types of conversations can occur during a break, in a private before or after business hours, or, depending on your role and your industry, you may be in a position to require an employee correction plan that includes assigning them to write a paper that clarifies their words or requires them to research their incorrect assumptions about the person or group of people they spoke poorly about. In some offices, it may be best to establish a planned protocol at the beginning of the company's creation or alter current onboarding and continuing education policies to indicate all rules and expectations that employees must follow, including non-discrimination and hostile work environment topic coverage.

When we look at the idea of safety, we must consider who is being kept safe. Politically, this can be a topic of significant debate. Often, this debate boils down to the difference between those who believe that people should not be forced to hear, see, or experience bigotry, and those who believe that shielding employees from this experience makes them ill-prepared to deal with the real world and the things that people may say in public spaces or during their careers. It can be easy for a conversation about safety to become a conversation and debate over one side or the other. However, this is not necessary, nor is it helpful to employees or business leaders.

This can lead to discussions about what safety measures are realistic. While some may feel that there should be significant opportunities for LGBT+ employees or employees of other minority groups to lead these conversations, this is not often possible. It is necessary as a leader to recognize that those in a position to make decisions about budgets may not be able to allocate programming or funds to one specific minority group within the business. However, it cannot be that nothing is done because action is said to be unaffordable. Instead, it is necessary to consider what changes and improvements can be made with little to no cost and with little to no change in the daily interactions of employees and staff. These recommendations are much more likely to be approved by those in positions of power because they cause very little, if any, upset to predetermined budgets or to how business leaders and employees typically behave.

Instead, business leaders can refer to existing business rules and policies. If there is already something in place regarding bullying, verbal assault, or physical assault, creating inclusion for LGBT+ people by making small changes becomes very simple. In some businesses, support for LGBT+ people would be listed as a separate item within the business rules and guidelines. In other businesses, they simply add the language "sexual orientation and gender identity" to rules that already list the types of bigotry or harassment that may exist, and which are not permitted. In today's society, most businesses already have policies in place regarding sexually explicit words and actions, as well as gender biases, so including "sexual orientation and gender identity" or replacing previous words with these can make this policy much more inclusive, with very little change. This can result in a reasonably quick alteration without significant discussion or concern by business leadership board or existing staff.

In addition to this set of rules being a requirement of employees to understand and follow, businesses typically mandate business leaders be mindful of the rules and be held accountable for following them. Usually, this is because businesses believe that business leaders are automatic role models and that following these rules is simply modeling appropriate adult behavior and interaction, which betters the business experience for everyone. It may be necessary to alert all staff in the district when a policy change is made or when additional words are added to existing policies. This allows everyone to recognize the change, and this will also enable business leaders and staff to be held accountable if they break these rules. These not only protect all LGBT+ employees, but they also protect LGBT+ business partners, and LGBT+ members of the community who may interact with the business through volunteer work, attending business or networking events, and/or those who advertise with the business in local school academic award programs, athletic sponsorship, or when donating for business events. This protection keeps everyone physically and psychologically safe from discrimination and bigotry in business settings and at business events.

Allyship

Why It Matters That You Are an LGBT+ Ally

Several business leaders may question whether there is a need for reading this book. These are typically either those who have personal feelings and beliefs about the LGBT+ community or those who already identify themselves as LGBT+ supporters. Those who have personal opinions and beliefs must recognize that it is against codes of conduct and professional codes of ethics to do less for one group of employees than another or to allow one's personal beliefs or opinions to negatively influence the experience that employees receive. It is also likely in the contract signed to commit to a leadership role within a company that there is something in the policy that prevents business leaders from adversely interacting with employees, staff, parents, and community members based on their minority status(es). This means that even if a reader of this book has powerful beliefs against the LGBT+ community or against employees who self- identify as LGBT+, it is not permissible to avoid this topic. Instead, the information within this book can help both those with negative beliefs with opposition and those who already identify as LGBT+ supporters to best understand how to use their platform as business leaders to provide the best possible environment and experience for all, including the LGBT+ community.

The idea of identifying as an ally of any marginalized group of people is not new. While many may consider themselves to be an "LGBT+ ally," there is significant difference across the spectrum of ally identities. For others, this book may require more introspection to identify how and why their personal beliefs, opinions, and actions may influence their treatment of LGBT+ employees, business staff, and business community leaders. Regardless of what identity a reader of this book wears, being mindful of that identity is not enough. Instead, we must examine what it means to be someone who supports the LGBT+ community, whether this is due to a personal conviction or mandates by the profession, the business district, and/or policies and laws.

This leads to questioning who qualifies as an ally. What makes a person qualified to identify as someone supportive of this community? This is something that may be debatable. In some cases, a person may identify themselves as an ally by simply not going out of their way to harm an LGBT+ person. Others may think that their ally status applies because they vote in each election in favor of inclusive policies. While neither of these is incorrect, and both benefit the LGBT+ community, this is not enough. Some debate whether the word "ally" is the best descriptor of a person regarding the LGBT+ community and their impact on it. While "ally" is the most commonly used word, some use the word "advocate," which implies much more of an active experience. To be an ally simply means to not go against this group of people. To be an advocate would acknowledge speaking up with or for LGBT+ people in situations where there may not be an LGBT+ person present, or where it may not be safe for an LGBT+ person to be out. Those who do more may be considered an "activist." Typically, this is a person who participates in different layers and levels of supporting the LGBT+ community. This may mean that the person talks with business boards or local, state, or federal politicians regarding better protections for LGBT+ people. In organizations that actively work to prevent equality for LGBT+ people, allies, advocates, and activists may be referred to as "accomplices." In the same way that a person who commits a crime may have an accomplice who helps them to commit a crime, the word "accomplice" is used to draw negative connotations to anyone who works to support the LGBT+ community.

Who Am I and What Traits Do I Bring to Allyship?

Often, the concept of being an ally is brought about in one of two ways, either as a passive construct "just don't behave in ways that harm a group of people" or in an aggressive construct "scream as loudly as possible when you observe bigotry or mistreatment." Typically, neither option feels like a fit for most people, leaving the majority to either be unclear how they can be an ally or to cause people to not know what to do and thus decide that it is better to do nothing than to do the wrong thing.

As you spend time learning and growing within the pages of this book, it will be important that you consider how you will engage with the material as you envision yourself utilizing what is taught. It is encouraged that you consider who you are and what traits come most naturally to you. Here are some descriptive words that may be how you see yourself and ways in which you may find it most natural for you to channel your new knowledge and your new role as an ally ...

First to speak up in a meeting, happy to share your ideas with leadership, excited by the chance to present at a conference

Your allyship may be loud and proud! You may find a desire to attend rallies, participate in protests, or you may seek out opportunities to sit on boards or committees at work or within your community to support inclusion. You might even decide to create programming in your workplace to measure the efficacy of more inclusion, with the plan to present your findings as an industry event where others may adopt your methods.

You may be seen as someone who speaks up and calls out disrespectful conversations and holds your colleagues accountable. LGBT+ people may see you as a safe person in the workplace because you never make them feel alone in moments when another employee is saying or doing something homophobic or transphobic. Your actions help LGBT+ employees feel seen, heard, and valued. It can be what lessens workplace bullying and may even save a life.

The go-to when something needs to be done right, always relied upon by others on the team, the boss' right hand

You may not be someone who speaks up in any format but your ability to put what you learn into practice is impressive! You'll be the one who uses the information within this book to inform your behaviors and you will naturally seek out ways to alter existing policies and procedures within your workplace.

You may be seen as someone who helps the boss to see where company culture can improve. It may be your voice in the boss' ear that helps them to reassess how the employees treat LGBT+ colleagues, ensuring that sexual and gender minorities do not become left out or ostracized in the workplace. Your actions help LGBT+ employees feel seen, heard, and valued. It can be what lessens workplace bullying and may even save a life.

Not a fan of team meetings but great one-on-one, more likely to write thoughts down than to voice them, more of an observer than a talker

When you hear or observe someone behaving badly or making comments out of ignorance, you excel in taking the person aside and helping them to see the errors in their ways without making them feel embarrassed! You might do this by using your words or by quietly giving them a copy of this book. You may be best able to be an ally by writing emails to decision-makers and lawmakers within your community and state. While you are not the first to speak up, you are often the wise one that others come to for guidance before making a company-wide change, making your allyship crucial to the collective.

You may be seen as the point person for new inclusion policies. Your ability to oversee groups of people and to observe without reacting may be what helps the entire office or company become more mindful of areas where they need to improve and ways in which LGBT+ people may be better included in the growth and goals of the company. Your actions help LGBT+ employees feel seen, heard, and valued. It can be what lessens workplace bullying and may even save a life.

Some of you may have found that you fit into more than one category, resulting in even more ideas and ways to be a supportive ally. Others of you may have noticed that, regardless of the behaviors that most likely fit your personality type and role, you were told that your actions help LGBT+ employees feel seen, heard, and valued. It can be what lessens workplace bullying and may even save a life. This is because there is no one way to be a great LGBT+ ally. Each of these actions helps. Each time you act helps. An LGBT+ person does not just need or deserve your support in the workplace once or twice, but all the time, until confirmed changes occur within the culture and the acceptable behaviors of everyone. The more you use your inherent gifts and talents to support someone in a way that feels most natural to you, the better the workplace is for every one of every background and identity. Your contribution to that experience not only aligns with compassion and strong leadership skills in that moment, but it may also reverberate throughout the workplace and may be long held in the heart of the person your words or actions supported.

How to Be an Active Ally

How do you let people know that you are supportive? This is something that is much more introspective. Although we've discussed when this support is mandated by your profession, by your professional association, and by the rules and regulations you agreed to in order to become a leader in your specific business, how you support and how you let people know that you support is much more personal.

This leads us to consider how much you will stand up in support of the LGBT+ community. Is there something you are willing to say, but if you get a certain amount of pushback, you will sit quietly? This can cause us to ask: What are you willing to risk? Is there a line for you regarding who you are willing to upset, or how much you are willing to speak up and where you could be silenced? This is not rooted in judgment; different people have different priorities.

In some cases, it might be less risky for a person who has additional income to speak more loudly in support of the LGBT+ community because they are not financially risking their ability to pay their bills. In other situations, a person may have to choose whether to risk being suspended or terminated at work to support the LGBT+ community. While this is not intended to create a hierarchy of support among you and your colleagues, this is an internal or even a family conversation you may wish to have in advance so that you can make these decisions during a time at home rather than in the middle of a debate or problem situation.

Another question to consider is whether you would be willing to accept the stigma that comes with an LGBT+ identity. Often, our society believes that people only fight for those who are like them. It can cause people to question the personal identity of allies, advocates, or activists working for any marginalized groups. However, it is often much easier to see a person not identifying with a group they support when this differentiation is visible and prominent. For example, a white person participating in a protest or discussion for Black Lives Matter does not at any time appear to be a person of color. Since identifying as LGBT+ is not always visually apparent, supporting this community may cause some to make assumptions about one's sexual orientation or gender identity. Thus, it is essential to consider how far you may be willing to go to support a community and at what point, if ever, you will feel the need to separate yourself from the community by making it clear to others that you are not a member of that community.

In some cases, this may feel like simply being honest or even showing others that this population deserves support and acceptance from everyone, not just from other LGBT+ people. In different situations, becoming vocal about one's own gender identity or sexual orientation becomes a way to lessen the risk or minimize any backlash of participation of support. Again, there may not be a correct answer, but this is something you may wish to think through or talk through before events occur in which decisions would need to be made on this topic.

Let's look at mistakes that are often made by those who do indeed mean well and are supportive of LGBT+ people. This is not intended to cause you to second-guess your support in the future, or to come down hard on yourself if you realize anything that follows may indicate a mistake you have made in the past. This is intended to shine a light on areas that may not have been highlighted and to provide new considerations for supportive behaviors moving forward.

Do you tell your colleagues if somebody identifies as LGBT+? Is this something that you tell because it is exciting gossip? Is this something that you discuss with the intention of preventing somebody from making a homophobic, biphobic, or transphobic comment in front of a person who identifies as LGBT+? While the aim here may be right, it is never appropriate to talk about a person's sexuality or their gender unless they have given you specific permission to do so. Although you may mean well, this can create situations in which safety may become an issue for an LGBT + person because there are some who do become violent, and because it means that the LGBT+ person does not know exactly who is aware of their identity. In addition, many states of America still allow a person to be fired for identifying as LGBT+. Even in cases where you think you are being helpful and where you absolutely mean well, outing an LGBT+ person at any time can put them at significant risk. Outing them in a workplace or to anyone who also works there can result in them losing their job. While this may not seem like a realistic situation because you know your colleagues, it is not always clear whose personal beliefs may cause them to create problems for an LGBT+ person.

Do you support equality specifically for the accolades and praise? While many people like to complete volunteer work or attend events in support of a minority group, it is essential to consider whether you would continue to support these organizations, people, and events even if you were never thanked, noticed, or praised for your support. Do you speak up when you hear bigotry? With its ongoing and consistent reports of violence against those in the LGBT+ community, the news has made it clear how frequently hate crimes occur. This means that anyone speaking up to support LGBT+ people in a public setting is taking a risk. This may be a minimal risk, or it may be more serious—for example, when involved in witnessing a violent act or some type of harassment against LGBT+ people. Do you have a line at which you stop supporting and stop helping? Acknowledging this in advance can help to prepare you for situations where you may have something occurring in front of you.

Too often, people do not think through what they would do in a situation until they are in that situation. That can lead to feeling uncertain of how to respond or not responding at all. In these situations, someone's safety may be directly threatened.

Knowing in advance how you would respond can help the person being victimized either because you choose to step in or because you are quickly able to find an alternative solution to help that person. Another consideration is whether and how much you would speak up in support of LGBT+ employees and colleagues when it comes to your own family. It is common for people to be willing to step up or speak up when something is occurring in a public space between strangers. This is often because right and wrong can appear obvious. Plus, many people are not very concerned with what a stranger may think if they speak up. However, what about your own loved ones? Do you speak up if your spouse or staff member says something against LGBT+ people in their workplace or business? Do you speak up at a holiday meal when someone in your extended family says something negative about LGBT+ people? Often, there are no clear-cut answers. However, this may be a conversation to have with those you are closest to in advance, or before a large family gathering. In some cases, it may not make sense to challenge a grandparent in the moment. However, you may make the decision to address it with that person and with others at a different time.

Being mindful of this before the event can help to prevent anyone from believing that your silence in the moment equals an agreement to what was just said. Finally, do you self-identify to make sure that bigoted people know that you are not an LGBT+ person? While it may be intentional to identify otherwise when participating in political conversations, attending pride parades, or otherwise choosing to show that non- LGBT+ people also support LGBT+ people, it is also worth examining if there are times when you may want to self-identify so that you are not mistaken for an LGBT+ person. This leads back to the self-conversation of where the line of activism and support is for you.

Now that you have considered the above areas for yourself, within your relationship, within your family, and within your professional capacity, it is also important to identify ways in which it is possible to do better and to do more. Although there may be more LGBT+ representation in the media than ever before, the number of LGBT+ hate crimes that occur each year continues to grow. But this is a statistic that can be reversed with increased career of diversity and inclusion, which can lead to acceptance and lower experiences of violence.

One way to improve is to listen to your LGBT+ employees and your LGBT+ colleagues. Being willing to hear the stories of LGBT+ people without interrupting them or turning the conversation back to you and your experiences allows that person to share their story and to feel heard as it is happening. While typical discussions are often a bit of a volley between participants listening and then sharing, specifically sharing experiences related to an LGBT+ identity can be very scary, especially for your newer employees, who may be trying to discern whether or not you are a safe person they can trust. If a person decides to share with you, understand that they are trusting you with something significant. This is not meant to be the same sort of conversation as if you were discussing favorite bands; it is instead a way that you are being asked to absorb and take in their experience.

Next, learn from those lessons being shared, knowing that your LGBT+ employees and LGBT+ colleagues are telling you something important. While it is common for people in majority groups to place the blame of negative interactions on minority members, listening to these stories can result in better understanding of how and why people are victimized. As is the case in any attack or victimization, it is never the victim's fault. It is never appropriate to ask a person why they didn't behave differently; it is instead necessary to validate that you have heard what they've shared, that you acknowledge their trust in you with a vulnerable part of themselves, and that you do not turn it into an opportunity to blame the victim for what someone else did to them.

Next, talk about it with others without outing the employee or colleague. When you are talking with others about the issues and stigma that LGBT+ people face, be sure to keep the stories that you tell of other people's lives vague enough so that you are not outing those who shared with you to new people. You can start with "I have an employee who ..." or "I heard about a leader at another business who ..." If the details of the story are something you find necessary to be heard by others, discuss this with the person who shared with you. Ask them if they would be open to sharing their story. Offer to go with them and sit by them if they agree to share their story. Or, if they are unwilling or unable, ask them if they would help you figure out what part of the story, they would feel comfortable with you sharing. This allows them to remain in control of their own experiences, their personal stories, and their own truth. Once you have received the information and experience that an LGBT+ person has shared with you, think about how you can use this new knowledge to help bring about more inclusion and better resolutions to minimize safety concerns.

Finally, donate your time and your support to your LGBT+ employees and colleagues. Find ways to use the resources that you have to support inclusive policies and supportive programming. This may be by offering to mentor an LGBT+ employee directly, by introducing an LGBT+ colleague to someone in your professional network who may be of help to their goals, or by talking with your workplace about what they can do to create more opportunities for LGBT+ employees to be groomed for leadership roles. (This is not to give LGBT+ people an unfair advantage, it is just much more likely for these situations to occur organically in majority groups and much less likely to occur in marginalized groups without intentional effort.)

Privilege

There has been a lot of discussion and debate about what privilege means, both as a term and how it impacts an individual's life. In reality, almost all of us have some modicum of privilege, whether overt or not. In fact, nearly all of us also have some situations in which we lack privilege. The point of acknowledging privilege is not to put down people who were or were not born a certain way or to blame people with privilege for having it. It is simply meant to lead to mindfulness. This allows a person to recognize the ways in which they benefit, which may not be something they regularly (or ever) consider.

What counts as privilege?

Anything that you get the benefit of that others do not counts as privilege. For example, if you can walk, talk, see, breathe, and eat on your own, there is privilege. If you live where there is not a war occurring, if you were taught to read, if you have access to sanitary supplies (including tampons/pads, toilet paper, soap, etc.) and clean water, there is privilege. If, in television and films, you see couples and love stories of people of your gender and the gender of people you are attracted to, there is privilege. If you identify as the gender that matches your genitalia, there is privilege. If you are young or classically attractive or financially stable or well fed or have air conditioning in your home or have a working vehicle or have access to medication when you are unwell or own books or watch television or have a smartphone or know how to drive or have a choice of clothing in your closet or sleep in a comfortable bed or consistently have electricity or bathe in warm water or have a consistent address, those are all privileges.

Why does privilege matter?

Too often, a conversation about privilege becomes an argument over who has more privilege than whom, which privilege is better to have than which other privilege, or what negative experiences counteract which privileges. This makes sense because it can be easy to assume that recognizing having privilege would be the same as claiming to have no problems or no right to complain about having problems. That's simply unrealistic and it can certainly inflame a conversation quite quickly. However, recognizing our privileges can help us to become more mindful of those who do not have what we have, as well as helping to articulate our needs to those who have what we do not.

For example, by recognizing that not everyone in your business location's community has consistent food access, a business or its staff member may become more aware of areas where wasted cafeteria food could be donated to those in need who may otherwise miss meals at home. By recognizing that the business may have not yet experienced a lawsuit by an LGBT+ employee for discrimination and your company having not yet been in the news for non-inclusive practices and policies means that the business can begin to examine areas in which improvement is needed, and there is an opportunity to make these changes before or without creating conflict or legal ramifications because of the poor experience of an LGBT+ person.

In short, the purpose of defining one's privilege as an individual, as a department, as a business, or as a business district is not to belittle or undermine occurring problems or stressors. It is simply to examine the ways in which the existing structure and schema benefit some while being detrimental to others. Once this awareness is obtained, it can be easy to begin to assess where there are areas that can be improved upon, which can lead to change, and which in turn can lead to a more inclusive and affirming business for all.

Intersectionality

Although the definition section is intended to be all- encompassing, it seems inappropriate not to provide a separate place to discuss and recognize intersectionality. Coined by Kimberlé Williams Crenshaw in 1989, the term identifies the intersection of being a member of more than one minority group. It recognizes that each group's membership comes with its own struggles and that the intersection of two or more memberships is more than simply the sum of society's mistreatment of each group within which a person identifies. The definition in this context is acknowledging that although an LGBT+ identity is, in itself, a minority status, many individuals exist within the intersection of two or more minority groups, which directly impacts their business experiences.

As one can imagine, each group that they are a part of causes them to be the target of misunderstanding and injustice, and to be at a higher risk of being victimized. The comic Wanda Sykes has built this into many of her comedy routines and interviews she has given, as she identifies as female, Black, and a lesbian. Her appearance allows the general public to assume her to be female and to identify her skin tone, leaving her already in a minority group at the intersection of female and Black. This individual exists at the intersection of female and Black and gay, creating three ways in which others may be biased against her, further causing her and others with this shared intersectionality to be that much more discriminated against than someone with only one of those three minority statuses, which is more discrimination than someone without any of these minority statuses faces.

In some cases, the identity of intersectionality may appear obvious. In other cases, there may be minority group status that may be more difficult for the casual observer to identify. In addition, there may be an assumption that certain members of certain minority groups may not identify as LGBT+. Typically, this occurs when one or more minority identifications lead the individual to be desexualized by society. One example of desexualized or infantilized groups is that of people with significant physical and/or learning disabilities. Through media portrayal and the additional need of assistance to perform daily tasks, it is common for society to see individuals with physical limitations as patients, as helpless, and/or as people to be pitied. This makes it difficult for many to recognize any gender identity or sexual orientation in association with that individual or an entire group of individuals with the same characteristics. This can result in a lack of representation for LGBT+ individuals who have obvious physical limitations. The deaf community is another group where members are often not considered to also be in a gender or sexual minority. While our society has been making strides to recognize that hard-of-hearing or deaf people live rich, full lives, it remains prevalent in the media that individuals of this minority group are seen as being in need of assistance or being victims of crimes.

Although this book focuses on making businesses more LGBT+ inclusive, this is not intended to be done at the detriment of recognition of other minority groups or their needs. Focusing on this particular group and its needs can also provide you with insights and tools to become more mindful of the needs of employees and staff who are part of other minority groups. Use what you gain via this book to encourage you to think about how different employees may need similar types of support and how you can be a more inclusive colleague.

Battle Fatigue

As you move through this book, giving yourself time to pause periodically and reflect, you are encouraged to consider not just how the information impacts your life and your actions but also how the lack of knowledge and the need to educate others has impacted LGBT+ employees, colleagues, and community leaders. Too often, a person in a minority group is expected to provide insights to others. There can be an expectation that it is incumbent upon a person in a persecuted group to raise their hand, explain their identity, explain how the current statement or situation is inappropriate, offer suggestions, recommend a solution, and implement the new course of action.

It is also necessary to consider that laws and law enforcement may already be against them. (This is not to discount areas where non-discrimination policies exist or the many wonderful police officers; this is simply to acknowledge how many areas of the nation lack even basic LGBT+ protections and how many stories exist where officers have been unkind or downright cruel to LGBT+ people.) There is also a significant amount of bigotry that exists, especially for those whose identities are at the intersection of a number of minority groups. This means that there may never be a time when the individual is able to truly relax because they are forced to always be in fear for their safety and their lives, spending a significant portion of their energy simply trying to stay alive before they can even begin to add other areas of focus to their day.

As such, it is easy for a person to become exhausted from trying to meet or manage the expectations others have of them, while being seen as the voice of their entire minority group and while trying to avoid becoming the victim of violence. For LGBT+ employees, their jobs become that much more difficult when they are not only at risk as people but even more so in areas where it is legal for them to be fired for their identity, which means that they consistently also live in fear of sudden job and income loss.

Supportive close professional friends, direct supervisors, and team members of LGBT+ people may also experience this fatigue. This is because may be forced to forever defend their person's identity to adults to ensure appropriate career opportunities and treatment in businesses, monitoring whether their peer or colleague is safe from bullying, and/or fending off those who mistreat them. This can result in significant and ongoing efforts by everyone to keep the LGBT+ person as safe and respected as possible.

As you move through this book and as you become more mindful of the experiences of LGBT+ people, you are encouraged to take time to think about when you personally have felt most unsafe, in danger, or at risk of violence. You are asked to think about how it felt when you were called down to the boss's office. You are asked to think about how your life would change if you were to be suddenly fired at this very moment. How would each of these situations feel?

As you consider each of these and the impact they would have on your life, you are encouraged to imagine the experience of living full-time in that feeling. You are asked to then consider how much additional strength it would take to feel this way and then complete your daily tasks and meet the expectations given to you by others. Finally, consider how it might feel if there was a person you could spend time with and a place you could go where those fears were lifted, where your safety was affirmed, and where your goals were supported. This is where you can begin to understand just how much of an impact you, your office, your business, and your business district can have on LGBT+ potential future employees, LGBT+ current employees, and LGBT+ colleagues.

Terminology

As we get ready to begin, people may be on very different levels of understanding about the topics of this book. Additionally, some people believe they understand more than they do, and others probably understand more than they think they do. In a desire for everyone to begin on the same page, let's start off talking about terminology so that we all move forward together through the rest of the book.

Before we begin with current knowledge, let's take a moment to discuss the history of the naming of this group of people. We used to see the abbreviation that GLBT (gay, lesbian, bisexual, transgender); now we typically see it as LGBT+ (lesbian, gay, bisexual, transgender). Why? Many women's groups argue that GLBT is yet another place where men are placed before women, so it is often considered more inclusive to place "lesbian" before "gay" as in "LGBT." However, as society and science begin to indicate that gender and sexuality may be more of a spectrum than a set number of boxes a person may check, it is becoming more common to see it listed as LGBT+. That allows for keeping the acronym short while also being the most inclusive possible.

All major medical and mental health professional organizations have long determined that inclusion, acceptance, and affirmation is what is best for LGBT+ people's health. This is really crucial because it considers the awareness that the LGBT+ population exists and why it exists, based on fact and on medical research. Too often, when talking about this population, there is an expectation that people's opinions should dictate how others are perceived. Instead, however, it is vital that we consider what professional associations say about this area in order to ensure that we are behaving based on best practices from science and research, rather than our own personal opinions, biases, or beliefs. (This is not to say that we can't acknowledge that we have our own opinions, biases, and beliefs; it is simply to indicate that although we have those, it is not our place as business leaders to impose them on others.)

When looking at this from a leader perspective, we have to consider the ways in which our own personal behavior toward and treatment of those who identify as LGBT+ may be hindering their ability to learn and fully contribute to the academic community of our business, business district, and overall community.

Let's look at appropriate terminology. This is something that does change often, so you may see some terms that used to not be accepted now being used, and you may also see that some terms that used to be accepted no longer are. Let's start with the umbrella terms first and then work into what falls under those umbrellas.

In Broad Terms

Sexual orientation: This refers to someone's sexual and romantic attraction. Most people have a sexual orientation. (Someone who does not is called asexual.) You can be attracted (romantically, emotionally, and/or sexually) to people of the opposite gender and identify as "straight" or "heterosexual," or be attracted to people of the same gender and identify as "gay" or "lesbian." You can also be attracted to people of either gender, which is called "bisexual." Some people identify as being attracted to a person regardless of their gender. This person would identify as "pansexual." Some people question whether a sexual experience is required for a person to know their orientation. Although each individual is unique, there are plenty of middle business and high business employees who identify their sexual orientation based on the feelings that they have, even if they have not had actual physical contact of a sexual nature.

Gender identity: Gender identity refers to a person's internal sense of being male, female, somewhere in between, or somewhere completely outside of the gender binary. For many people, one's gender identity corresponds with their biological facts; in other words, a person has female genitalia, and female DNA, and they identify as female. That makes the person cisgender. On the other hand, a person who identifies as transgender is someone who has external genitalia and DNA that do not match how that person sees themselves and how they identify in the world.

Gender expression: Gender expression relates to how a person chooses to communicate their gender identity to others through their clothing, hairstyles, manners, and behaviors. This may be conscious or subconscious. While most people's understanding of gender expression relates to masculinity and femininity, the expressions of these can occur in a myriad of ways, typically related to the impact of product marketing, mass media, and gender norms that date back generations. This is why we identify things like lace and glitter as being feminine and things like leather as being more masculine. Some people may choose an item specifically to broadcast their gender identity, and others may choose it because they enjoy it or like the way it feels, even if it does not necessarily correlate with their gender identity.

To summarize, sexual orientation describes who you feel sexually/romantically/emotionally attracted to. Gender identity is the gender that you feel in your brain regardless of your genitalia. Gender expression is what clothing, hairstyle, and mannerisms your conscious or subconscious mind chooses when you present yourself to the world.

Now that we've covered the overarching umbrella terminology, let's look at the terminology under these umbrellas.

Sexual Orientations

Gay: A man who is romantically and sexually attracted to other males. This may also be used as a term that is more inclusive which would encompass gay men, lesbians, and people who identify as bisexual.

Lesbian: A woman whose romantic and sexual attraction is to other women.

Bisexual: A person who is sexually/romantically/emotionally attracted to both men and women, though not necessarily simultaneously. A bisexual person may not be attracted equally to both genders, and the degree of attraction may change over time.

Lesbians

It should not be assumed that lesbians have never been sexually active with men; we cannot assume when talking with employees at middle business or high business that they have not had sexual encounters with males. Making this assumption can leave them unsafe due to lack of information given, because there is an assumption that information is not useful. The risks of suicidal ideation, self-harm, and depression may be higher in lesbians and bisexual individuals, especially those who are not open about their sexual orientation, who are not in satisfying and safe relationships, and/or who lack social support. Smoking and obesity rates are also higher in lesbians and bisexual women because smoking and eating are inexpensive ways in which some cope, and this population may be more likely to need coping mechanisms to deal with the stress of living in a world that is often homophobic and biphobic.

In addition, many lesbian and bisexual women are victims of hate crimes, and they often fear for their safety. Intimate partner violence may also occur between women in same-sex relationships at a rate that is similar to heterosexual relationships. Lesbian women can also be raped, physically assaulted, or stalked by a female partner. It may be difficult for employees to be open about this, especially if they do not feel supported at home and within the business. They may struggle with addressing these concerns and their relationships out of fear that they will not be believed, or that people will assume that women cannot be as violent toward each other as men have been known to be violent in interactions with women. If an employee comes to you with concerns about relationship safety, it is necessary that you follow the same protocol the business has for opposite-sex relationships and for any report of violence whatsoever.

Gay and MSM

This categorizes male-identified people who have sexual encounters and/ or relationship with other male- identified people. At the present time, some see "gay" as an identity that deals with a specific type of personality or type of behaviors. In those cases, some do not identify as "gay" but rather as "MSM"—men who have sex with men. (This may be how a male-identified employee identifies his sexuality, even if his age and/or appearance do not yet make him a "man" by definition.) Regardless of a person's chosen label, there is still an increased risk for this population of sexually transmitted infections (STIs) as well as psychological and behavioral disorders related to their experiences and whether or not they are accepted at home. It may be easy to find statistics that indicate that gay men or men who have sex with men are contracting more STIs than other groups; however, this research is often heavily biased either in the way the study was written to bolster pre-existing misperceptions or by misinterpreting the results to further a person or group's agenda, regardless of the breadth of research that indicates otherwise.

This may be because the people funding the study have personal or religious feelings about homosexuality. It may be because a drug company is biased in their studies in an attempt to indicate a need for a drug they are trying to sell. It may also be that the place in which these studies occur is heavily biased toward or against one type or group of people. For example, doing a study while inside a nightclub will likely only capture the responses of people who go to nightclubs; it will not also include people who do not go to nightclubs, which may be a significantly different experience. This detail is important to know, so that you can both consider your own biases and beliefs and have an understanding that parents of employees may make assumptions based on biased research that can cause them to be not accepting and not affirming of their employees. With this in mind, homosexuality has been associated with a higher risk of psychological and behavioral disorders, including depression, anxiety disorders, suicidal thoughts, and plans, eating disorders, alcohol and substance abuse, and cigarette smoking. The stigmatization of homosexuality in American society results in the frequent exposure of homosexual men to discrimination and victimization. This is believed to be a causative factor in the development of psychological and behavioral disorders.

Bisexual

In bisexual people, it is a common misconception that a person who identifies as bisexual is either "greedy" or uncertain. Others believe that a person identified as bisexual is actually gay, but they are not yet ready to admit that. This is inaccurate. There has been no single pattern to prove this assumption. Some bisexual-identified people feel they fit into neither the heterosexual nor homosexual world, while others feel identified more predominantly as being attracted to one gender identity than the other. Due to a lack of understanding, acceptance, or even knowledge of the bisexual identity, the failing relationship issues facing bisexual people seldom emerge when contemplating policy and legal changes. Some bisexual people have legally married opposite-sex partners. As a result, they are able to access the privileges afforded to married couples. However, many bisexual people are not married. They may choose not to get married, or their family may not be accepting of their union. Some may wish to become parents regardless of their marital status. Bisexual people often face similar discrimination and obstacles to those faced by gay and lesbian people in regard to issues of identity respect by society, as well as the impacts of dating, divorce, and child custody, visitation, or adoption of children. This means that in addition to your employees possibly identifying as bisexual, you may have employees who are dealing with additional traumas related to romantic relationships and/or the legal impact this may have on their family.

Not only is this something employees are learning about as they become clearer in their own sexuality, but this may also be impacting the custody agreements about them if the parents have already been divorced, or it may lead to parents being divorced. It is necessary to be respectful of this and to be mindful that this may be an aspect of the employee's personal life which may impact their behaviors and their abilities in the office, not because they do not care or because they are too lazy to complete their work, but because they may have these trials going on at home which may be too much of a distraction and emotional burden to manage while being able to complete all of their professional expectations on time.

Greysexual and Asexual

Greysexual is the limited capacity or low-level impact of sexual desire. This does not mean that the person does not or cannot feel romantically attracted to someone or that they are unable to build an emotional or intellectual connection with them. It simply means that they do not feel a significant or strong desire for sexual connection. Some still engage in sexual behaviors as they may see this as a compromise, they make for a partner they love, or they may be interested in engaging in these behaviors very infrequently. However, this is not something that motivates them.

Asexuality is the absence of sexual desire. This does not mean that the person does not or cannot feel romantically attracted to someone or that they are unable to build an emotional or intellectual connection with them. It simply means that they do not feel a desire for sexual connection. Some still engage in sexual behaviors as they may see this as a compromise, they make for a partner they love. However, this is not something that motivates them.

Gender Identity

People generally experience gender identity and sexual orientation as two different things. Sexual orientation refers to one's sexual attraction to others, whereas gender identifies a reference to one's sense of oneself in their own identity. Usually, the gender that the individual is attracted to does not change when a person begins to live openly as a transgender person. For example, a person assigned male at birth who is attracted to women will be attracted to women after transitioning, when they openly identify as female. This will mean that this person who was once seen by society as a heterosexual man would now be seen by the world as a lesbian.

Let's talk about gender! In present-day American society, there is an overarching norm that gender is binary—that is, that there are two options (male or female). This is decided based on external genitalia.

This is what is announced at "gender reveal parties," as it is based on whether the fetus does or does not have a penis. Sex and gender are not the same thing. Sex is the chromosomal designation of a person's genetics, whereas gender is a social construct. In other words, it should be called a "sex reveal party," since no one will know how the staff member identifies their gender for some time yet!

How is gender guided by society? This begins before a person is even born. It includes when people ask whether the baby is a boy or a girl. It includes when parents begin to envision their child's future extra-curricular activities (football or ballet, fixing cars or going shopping). It is often used to decide themes for baby showers, to send baby gifts, and to decorate nurseries. Pink and lace for girls; blue and trucks for boys. Check out the baby and staff member aisles in stores and you'll see this on full display; lace and ruffles for girls, reinforced knees on pants for boys. Hair and makeup toys in pink packages for girls; wrestling action figures and superheroes in blue packages for boys. In the tween and teen sections of stores, girls' areas are often filled with sparkly jewelry, whereas boys' sections have items meant not to stain easily. Everywhere you look, society shows that girls must be petite, delicate, and appearance-based, and boys are meant to be rough and tumble. While this may not be news to you, have you ever considered that society is also showing that there are only two genders?

What is gender? Gender is the way a person identifies their place in a spectrum of masculine and feminine, or outside of that spectrum altogether. How do people identify themselves within this spectrum?

Transgender

A broad term meaning that a person's gender identity does not match their assigned gender at birth.

Cisgender

A term to describe a person whose gender identity does match their assigned gender at birth. This means that transgender and cisgender are opposite terms.

Gender non-binary

A term to describe a person who identifies as a gender that is not male or female but may be a combination of the two or something different. (You may hear this abbreviated as "NB" and/or see this abbreviated in writing as "enby"—the phonetic pronunciation of NB. As the abbreviation of "NB" has long been in use in communities of color to indicate "non-Black," "enby" is the most inclusive written form of abbreviation for non-binary.)

Gender fluid

A term to describe a person whose gender identity may change or evolve over time. This goes beyond a desire to wear a dress one day and pants the next, as this is not about gender expression and clothing or hairstyle but rather about the identity of a person and how they are in their gender from day to day.

Agender

A term to describe a person who does not identify as having a gender.

These identities are also why we have added the + to the LGBT+ in our language, and why you will typically see more recent publications or speeches referring to this population as LGBT+.

Note: Transgender, cisgender, gender non-binary, gender fluid, and agender are adjectives, not nouns. Just like Black, Asian, Hispanic, short, and tall. There is no such word as "transgendered," as the word is not a verb, so it cannot have a past tense. Always put the word "person" after the gender-identifying word, as this is a word to describe someone. This is just the way you don't see a "short," you see a "short person." You may see the term "male to female transgender person" or "female to male transgender person." This has been used for quite some time to first identify the person's gender assigned at birth and second identify the gender the person identifies as. For example, a "male to female transgender person" would indicate that the person was assumed by others to be a male person at birth (due to external genitalia) and now identifies and/or lives as a female person.

However, updated terminology has also caused some to redefine the categorization of transgender people because science is indicating that gender is being seen more and more as a social construct. This would mean that nobody is born with a gender, since nobody is born with an innate sense of social construct. With that in mind, the terminology is being changed. Now, the identity of a transgender person is typically described as "assigned female at birth" (AFAB) or "assigned male at birth" (AMAB).

Medical options for transgender people: This is a conversation that is necessary because business leaders may see the results of some of these different actions and choices in the transgender population within their business, whether with an employee, staff member, or parent in the business's community.

Some mistakenly believe that medical options are easily acquired and happen quickly. In America, to be able to receive any medical intervention, the person must be consistently seen by a licensed mental health professional for many months or years, working in concert with a medical professional or team before any medical interventions can occur. In addition, health insurances do not typically cover any of these interventions, so many families spend years saving money to afford what is best for the individual. This means that although something may seem sudden to you, by the time you are aware of the change the family and individual have likely spent years being guided by multiple healthcare professionals. No one takes this lightly, and no medical interventions are offered or are an option until/unless multiple specifically trained gender professionals have done their work to ensure that this is the appropriate treatment for the person.

Not all transitions look the same.

(This will come up again when having conversations later in this book about restrooms and other ways in which employees and leaders should be mindful so that transitioning employees are not discriminated against intentionally or accidentally.)

Some may have transitioned from a young age while others may be helping their child through the transitioning process. This may cause them to have questions for your company regarding healthcare coverage. It may also impact whether they need to attend medical appointments with their child during the workday. This is because puberty blockers may be utilized in a child's or teen's transition. This is a type of medication that prevents the body from beginning or fully completing adult puberty. This means that people assigned male at birth will not grow facial and body hair, their voice will not deepen, and their genitals will not grow. For a person assigned male at birth who identifies as female, this is vital. If not given puberty blockers, a person identifying as a girl would have to watch her body become increasingly more male in appearance. This can create extreme anxiety and depression. It may even result in suicide attempts. For people assigned female at birth, puberty blockers prevent the body shape from changing at a time when hips would become wider and breasts would begin to grow. This can make a person who identifies as male become incredibly uncomfortable and feel unsafe in a body that is growing increasingly dissimilar to their gender identity. It can be a very unsafe time for a transgender person if puberty blockers are not provided. Though the majority of your staff may be adults, this may also impact youth volunteers, younger staff in the workplace as well.

When transitioning begins, in addition to blocking the puberty hormones that are not congruent with gender identity, hormones will begin to be introduced that encourage the body to develop in a way that aligns with the person's identity. This means beginning testosterone for people assigned female at birth who identify as male. That testosterone will do what it does in cisgender male teenagers: it will cause the voice to deepen, facial and body hair to begin to grow, and all other male physical characteristics to begin to develop. For employees assigned male at birth, the hormone introduced is estrogen, which allows for a more feminine shape, the raising of the voice pitch, and for breasts to begin to grow. In situations in which employees identify as transgender before puberty and have affirming and supportive parents, the use of puberty blockers followed by gender-confirming hormones can result in a staff member that appears to the public to be the gender in which they identify, though their genitalia may not match. In situations in which the family and/or colleagues are not affirming, these employees may become increasingly unsafe and this can increase the risk of self-harm or suicidality. Some may attempt to remove genitalia, and others may seek out illegal hormone blockers or hormone replacements in hopes of preventing their body from changing due to their natural hormones. In situations in which parents are not affirming, while hormone blockers and new hormones cannot simply be provided by the business, it will be necessary that business leaders be very mindful of the mental health of these employees and work with them to make plans in order to ensure their safety.

(Later, this book will guide you toward setting up a safer workplace, as these workers may struggle with being bullied by peers who are aware that they are transgender, even if the employee presents as the gender in which they identify.)

Although it is common that people are interested in this type of hormonal impact on someone, it is never ever okay to ask a person to disclose what hormones, if any, they may be taking. The only reason for this to be asked/ known is if the human resources office is inquiring specifically to meet an individual's medical needs regarding insurance plans, or if the person chooses to volunteer this information. While it is normal and typical for people to be interested, especially those who lack insight into this process, it is not the employee's role to educate their colleagues or supervisors. Instead, refer to this book and its resources to find out more without creating a situation in which the individual feels obligated to disclose or unsafe.

In addition, for general knowledge purposes and because many companies interact with the children of employees and/or host student interns, surgeries are probably not happening at the under K-12 school age group. This is because their bodies are still changing and growing, and most surgeons are not likely to perform a surgical procedure of any sort on anyone under the age of 17.

However, it is possible or even likely that among local or national or even international colleagues, there will be those who identify as transgender. They may have or may not have had any type of hormonal intervention or surgeries. This may include genital reconstruction surgery (typically referred to as gender confirmation surgery, though this terminology does change frequently); breast implants; the shaving down of an Adam's apple; a brow lift and shaving of the brow bone, or another surgery to feminize the face of a person assigned male at birth; or fat injections, breast reduction or chest reconstruction, and other options for people to appear more masculine for those assigned female at birth. Some identify a part of their body as not being congruent with their identity and thus want to make changes as quickly as medically possible. Others simply do not connect those aspects of their body to being related to gender the way that many do. At no time is it ever appropriate to ask about which surgeries, if any, a person has had. The only people who need to know that information are the person and their medical practitioners.

Those whom you work with, from interns to CEOs may be at any aspect of their transition. Do not make assumptions based on their age, on your location's laws, on the media, or on how the individual appears to you.

A transgender person is not "more trans" or "less trans" based on how far through a transition process the person is. Some people choose never to take hormones and never to have surgery, others only choose to utilize some of the treatment options, and others choose to alter their physical appearance without utilizing any hormonal or surgical options. This is a personal choice based on their own feelings about their bodies and based on financial options available.

Some people believe that they can identify a transgender person simply by looking at them. While this might have been largely true in past generations because there was no opportunity to utilize hormones and surgical options, the idea that this is an obvious identity is incredibly outdated, and the imagery that people use is incredibly biased. There are many people who identify as transgender, gender non -conforming, or gender non -binary whose appearance may give no indication of their gender identity. It is not their obligation to provide this information to you. You may have access to this information if the business listed the employee under one name and gender, but the person presents and identifies differently. In these cases, make sure to communicate with your supervisor in order to make sure that the name and pronouns within the office for the person are what they have asked to be called. You may also wish to speak with your supervisor about changing the name and pronoun on the attendance sheets and any computer programming in order to ensure that the person is not misgendered or misnamed in places where they or others consistently see this information. Remember that a transgender person is just like any other person; their bodies and their choices with their bodies are none of your business unless you are a medical professional and the question you are asking is medically necessary. While you may have questions, it is not the individual's job to teach you, nor is it appropriate for you to expect such. If, however, you are unsure, ask the employee privately and follow their lead. Never ask a person of any age about this information or anything related to their identity in front of others. It is already very difficult for transgender people of all ages to avoid bullying or violence and putting the spotlight on their identity in front of others may make the situation much harder for them.

Some associate the idea of a transgender person with being a drag queen. They're very, very different. Drag queens and drag kings are biological males and females respectively who present as members of the other sex specifically to perform or entertain. The performance may include singing, lip-synching, or dancing. Drag performers may or may not identify as transgender. Many drag queens and kings identify as gay, lesbian, or bisexual. This is very different from a transgender person; whose heart and mind are of a gender that is different than their genitalia and who is living as themselves. Transgender people do not do this for the entertainment or amusement of others; it is simply who the person is. As an example, this is the difference between the way you may choose to dress up for Halloween and your identity every day; one is meant to be fun and entertaining, and the other simply is who you are.

While it used to be very rare for anybody to openly identify as LGBT+, the past decade has significantly changed this. Members of boy bands including members of New Kids on the Block and *NSYNC have come out as gay. Sonny and Cher's son has come out as a transgender man, living openly, and with the support of his parents. Top musicians have also identified themselves as bisexual, or lesbian, taking their partners with them to very public events. This can be incredibly helpful and affirming for those in the LGBT+ community; however, the social change of people feeling more able to be out and live openly does not mean that bullying does not happen. In order to prevent bullying in the business and in general, allies are necessary.

When looking at estimates for how many LGBT+ people there are in any given city, state, or country, it is very difficult to accurately account for this. This is because there is often bias in the accounting experience, and it also requires a person not only to be out but also to trust the survey taker with this personal information. This can lead to statistics that are much lower than are actually accurate in terms of how many people identify as LGBT+ in America today.

When working with a transgender employee, a few tips:

Number one, it isn't always about the employee's transgender status. It is important not to focus so narrowly on the fact that a person is transgender that you end up making that characteristic more important than the actual reason the employee is seeking your help or support or insight or guidance. It is important that you help your employee focus on the real issue and steer them away from focusing on their gender identity if that is not the core problem. For example, if a transgender employee is struggling with a marketing question, it is important to focus on the marketing question or to discuss how to better train the employee on the marketing skills they need in order to do their job well. It would make sense in some cases to be mindful that the staff member may have some additional struggles simultaneously due to their gender identity. However, it is also very likely that this is an employee simply struggling with marketing, just the way so many cisgender employees do. By focusing on marketing concerns, it allows the employee to be guided appropriately without ignoring the real issue of marketing difficulty, and without letting the employee off the hook for making marketing mistakes due to their transgender identity.

Second, be aware of the assumptions you are making about a person's gender. It is very common to assume that you know a person's gender or gender identity based on stereotypes. Some people's expression or identity is not stereotypical and may be different from what you would expect or assume. Therefore, it is important to be open to allow a person to self-identify. If you are unsure, it is appropriate to ask the person how they would like to be addressed. Often, this can be taken care of easily on the first day of business. Just as when you meet an employee for the first time and give them the opportunity to identify the name they prefer to be called, the same can be true for transgender employees. Just as an employee named Elizabeth would tell you on the first day of business that she prefers to be called Liz or Lizzie or Beth, it is equally appropriate for an employee named David to tell you that she prefers to be called Denise. Just as you would write that Elizabeth has asked to be called Liz, you should do the same for a transgender employee so that all employees in your office are spoken to and called by the name that they go by. This allows for inclusive offices without doing anything that singles out a transgender employee. You will also want to ensure that any email address, name plate on an office door/cubical, in the company directory, on staff name badges, and anywhere else where their name will be displayed.

It is also important to be mindful of orientation assumptions. While most employees do identify as heterosexual, not all do. This means that if an employee is talking about someone they are dating, do not assume that the employee is speaking of someone of a different gender. Making these assumptions or making jokes in meeting may seem light and fun but they could put a target on an employee who needs to lie about their life for the meeting to move on or may cause them to feel as if they are in an office where it may not be safe. Instead, you can simply remind all employees that talking about their date on Friday night is not a conversation meant to be happening in the middle of your meeting and encourage them to focus and get back to work, just as you would any other employee talking about any other date.

It is also important to know the laws. This is a constantly changing situation. While this is not always something that everyone can keep up with, it may make sense in your business for the supervisor or principal to assign one person whose job it is to be mindful of changes. This can create a protocol in which legal changes can be sent by email to the entire staff so that everyone is aware. In addition, if you live in a state in which the laws are less than inclusive and respectful, this does not require you not to be inclusive or respectful. You can always curate the business system, a business building, and/or your office to be a place in which an employee can be authentically themselves.

Next, except in rare cases, it is very important that you use the name and the pronoun that corresponds to that person's gender identity. In addition, your employee may choose to use a name that is gender-neutral or associated with the opposite gender for the pronoun; it is important to be aware of and respect this. This may mean that someone named Brian prefers to be called Brian but uses female pronouns. This may mean that your employee prefers to be called Sam—a name that does not distinguish their gender—just like Elizabeth prefers to be called Liz. Just like Elizabeth preferring to be called Liz, simply marking this in all company listings and on all staff name badges and directories reminds you always to call on them using the name they have asked to be called, showing respect to the employee.

(Transgender-friendly policies in this book will discuss what that means, how to create them, and what to do if others in your business are less welcoming.)

As we move forward in this book, there may be situations that feel unrealistic because the people in your community are not inclusive, or those who explore related decisions are not inclusive. You are not being asked to go directly against what your supervisors say, but nothing prevents you from being someone who is aware of the knowledge and science related to the LGBT+ community. Nothing prevents you from being someone who is welcoming, and nothing prevents you from letting your employees know that homophobic, biphobic, and transphobic language is never okay in your office.

Additional Useful Terminology

Microaggression

Subtle, indirect, or unintentional discrimination against someone for their identity. Often, individuals use microaggressions to let someone in a marginalized group know that they are unwanted or unwelcome while still being able to feign cluelessness if they are confronted about their behavior. In other cases, microaggressions can occur when unintended ignorance leads a colleague to make a comment that is well-meaning but is inappropriate and offensive. A business-wide refusal to ignore microaggressions or second guess a person who reports them helps to lessen their frequency. An employee or leader who consistently works to learn about marginalized groups (such as by reading this book) helps to lessen the likelihood of accidental microaggressions.

Homophobia

The intense fear and hatred of or discomfort with people who love and are attracted to members of the same gender.

Transphobia

The intense fear and hatred of or discomfort with people whose gender identity or gender expression does not match or conform to cultural gender norms.

Internalized Homophobia or Transphobia

When self-identification of societal stereotypes results in a person hating who they are, causing them to dislike or resent their sexual orientation or gender identity.

Coming Out

What does "coming out" or "coming out of the closet" mean? It is the process of telling another person that you are LGBT+. There has been talk for decades about famous people coming out. Celebrities do it on the covers of magazines, singers do it at concerts or via their music videos, and some social media stars post entire videos of themselves coming out to their loved ones. In many areas of the country, the expectation is that of an immediate happy moment; an LGBT+ person hesitantly and fearfully tells someone they care about, and the person immediately embraces them and talks about how love knows no limits. In fact, it can be seen as homophobic/biphobic/transphobic if the person reacts any other way. While there is a lot to unpack in terms of the coming-out experience within families, let's focus on the experience and its importance within a business setting.

When an employee comes out at any age, they are choosing to let their peers and the business mentors know something very personal about them. If an employee comes out to you, this can be a surprise, and that surprise can lead to an uncomfortable or awkward interaction. As such, it can be better for business leaders and staff to think through the process generally, so they are at least somewhat prepared when the situation occurs in the future.

If a colleague comes out to you

It is important to keep the focus on the employee. Your personal thoughts, feelings, or opinions about LGBT+ people, coming out, or that employee are not relevant in that moment. Instead, be mindful that the employee is trusting you with information that speaks to their identity. Interns and employees at the lowest positions in your company are growing and developing into future industry leaders, and their sense of self and sense of self-worth is very malleable at this time. Your reaction and response can help or hinder their mental health and their self-confidence. As such, you may choose to thank them for sharing this. If the adult is coming out as a different gender, it may be appropriate to ask them if they would like you to call them by another name or use different pronouns. You might also wish to let them know that you accept them and that they can come to you any time they are in need of support.

You may want to inquire into who else knows. Here, you may glean information about whether the news is common knowledge among their peers, whether they have chosen to share this information with others at work, and how their home life is going. Remember that, unless there is a safety concern, it is never your place or your right to share this information with others. This is not a silly personality quirk that is fair game to joke about with the employee; this is not gossip for the break room; this is not a topic to discuss at business conferences. Employee safety and privacy must be a priority, especially in a situation where sharing this information can lead to discrimination, bullying, or self-harm. If you think the employee may be at risk of being harmed or harming themselves, follow standard safety protocols. However, be sure to find out beforehand whether the person or people who are involved in creating these protocols (those in the Human Resources department or those in any Employee Assistance Program offered) are affirming and accepting. You want to guide the employee to get the help they need; you do not want to refer them to someone who will further the problem. If you find that there is no one in that position to refer the employee to, reach out to a state or national hotline for LGBT+ issues, and they can guide you toward the best option for employee safety in this situation.

Allow the employee to guide the conversation and to end it when they feel they are done sharing. You can periodically check in with them privately and keep an extra eye out for any slip in their work or negative comments from peers. However, your treatment of the employee should otherwise not change from before they came out to you. The goal is not to treat them as either less or more than their peers; it is simply to ensure their safety and to be an affirming person for them within the business.

Although it is common for the assumption to be that coming out is a stressor only for developing adults whose peers can be rude or downright cruel, the coming-out experience for adults can also be stressful. Coming out to a work colleague can be even more anxiety-inducing. Although there are legal protections to keep a person from being fired for being LGBT+, this does not mean that every workplace is accepting, affirming, or kind to LGBT+ people. As a result, letting a coworker know something personal can feel like opening the door to be judged, ridiculed, or mistreated. It is vital that you respond with kindness and support.

If someone who reports to you comes out to you

Let the staff member know that you value them, and you appreciate their choice to trust you with this information. If they are alerting you to a difference in gender identity, ask if they would like you to call them by another name or to use different pronouns. You can also ask for additional guidance on how you can best support them. Just as with employees coming out, this information is highly personal and should never be discussed with others unless a safety concern is present. If there is such a concern, find out the protocol set up by your business. In many cases, there is an employee assistance program hotline you can call with questions. Be sure to keep the colleague's name anonymous while researching how to help, in order to protect their privacy. Just as with an employee situation, if you are unsure whether a referral is to someone accepting, reach out to a state or federal LGBT+ help hotline for guidance.

Questions and Answers

Q: How do I know what to call someone if I think they might be LGBT+?

A: If you aren't sure what name to call someone, ask for their name, and they'll tell you. This is the same for any person whose name you forgot. This is also the same for someone who was named Carter Joel, who prefers to be called CJ. This isn't something specific to the LGBT+ community, although many feel anxious out of fear of offending a person in the LGBT+ community. In this case, when it comes to someone's name, it is just the same as anyone else's name, but you do not know, do not remember, or cannot recall what version of their name they may choose to go by.

Q: What about pronouns? How do I know whether to use he or she or ...?

A: If you are uncertain about pronouns, ask, "What pronouns do you use?" It is considered most appropriate to ask the question that way, rather than to ask, "What is your preferred pronoun?" This is because "preferred" indicates that this is about preference and not about identity. You're not asking a person which version of a pronoun they might prefer, like the way you may ask me if I prefer chocolate or vanilla ice cream and I might like one more than the other. Instead, you are asking what pronoun they use, just the way that someone might ask what racial background you are or height you are; this is not what a person prefers—it is who they are. You may hear someone introduce themselves with their name, followed by the pronouns they use. For example, when a person introduces themselves and includes their pronouns, they may say, "Hi, I'm Rachel, she, her, hers." That means that their name is Rachel, and they identify using female pronouns. If you were to tell someone that this person agreed to go to the store, you would say, "Rachel said she can go to the store." If you said, "Rachel said he can go to the store," that would not feel right to them, and it would not be a fit with how they identify.

Some prefer to use a pronoun that is neither male nor female. The introduction to such a person would sound like, "Hi, I'm Melvin, they, them, theirs." On many computer programs, this will be underlined as a mistake because "they" and "theirs" are known to have been plural, and you are using the pronoun for one individual person. This may require you to correct your word processing program. This is because the English language has not yet offered a singular non-binary gender pronoun, although this is common in many other languages. However, the Merriam-Webster dictionary now accepts they/them/their as singular pronouns too.

Research Your Resources

Although the workplace may theoretically be only a place where work occurs, in reality, many workers spend more time in the office and with colleagues than in their homes with their families. As a result, it is likely that a business leader will spend significant time getting to know those they work with. This may include experiences related to celebrations of marriages, births, and career advancement. It is also realistic that it may include knowing when an employee is struggling or suffering in their personal life. In most business settings, there is a general awareness among staff regarding community resources for those in need. For example, if an employee or staff member becomes combative or violent, the police are called. If there is an injury beyond the purview of the office's first aid kit, the paramedics are called, and the person is taken to the hospital. If a staff member is unexpectedly in need of a home or food, they are referred to local homeless shelters, food pantries, and donation services. Sounds familiar, right?

But what if those referrals exacerbate the problem or put the person at higher risk of injury or mistreatment?

Safety and Medical Emergencies on Business Grounds

As you continue through the process of becoming more aware of the needs of LGBT+ people in your business community, take the time to research the organizations and resources that are commonly utilized (or even mandated by protocol). Find out whether the police and paramedics have been trained to treat LGBT+ people and, if they say they are, ask for information about what that training entails and whether it is mandated to everyone. Reach out to the local hospital or hospitals and find out about their policies and training programs for LGBT+ patients and families. Ask about specific support offered and skills training for this specific population. In addition, consider what information these professionals would request or require from the business in the event of an emergency situation. Are your business records up to date? How quickly are they changed to include gender identity or name changes, as needed? What are your business's rules on how much information is provided, and what are considered protected details of an employee or staff member's life?

Health and Wellness Concerns at Home

Over your years or decades working in businesses, it is likely that you will encounter many employees whose families are struggling financially. This may occur for a variety of reasons that are incredibly common. It may also occur if an adult in the family is LGBT+ identified, as this population is consistently underpaid and struggles to find and maintain employment in areas where discrimination against LGBT+ people remains legal. Regardless of what causes a family not to have enough money to cover all of their living expenses, these situations do happen. As such, you are likely to encounter situations where a family may be or become homeless and/or food -insecure. They may need assistance in purchasing business supplies and clothing. It is likely that your business already has a document prepared with a list of local homeless shelters, food pantries, and thrift or free stores. However, not every organization is accepting and affirming of LGBT+ people. Some use their religious affiliation as the reason they are not accepting. Others claim to have values that are based on their founder's upbringing many generations ago. Whatever the reasoning, it is not helpful to the family to refer them somewhere where they will be ridiculed and/or turned away when they are most in need of support.

Take the time to review and research the locations on the existing list. Look into the overarching organizations that fund or sponsor each program. Seek out information about how families are kept together in homeless shelters and whether this changes if the family has same-sex parents or a transgender person in their family unit. Find out whether the organizations' mission statements include religion of any sort and, if so, contact them to inquire about how staff and volunteers are trained to interact with LGBT+ people. You may find that there is little or no guidance given, allowing each worker to decide whether to welcome a family in or whether to turn them away for somehow living a life that goes against the organization's expectations or beliefs.

In some cases, businesses may have a volunteer or community group that gathers neighbors and community leaders to put together care packages for families who cannot afford many basic items that local community need. These can be a great way to bring folks together and provide a sense of support and care within the community. However, you may also need to inquire into the practices and protocols of these groups as well as other local or federal organizations that donate holiday toys, business supplies, or clothing in regard to how they proceed when a person's gender identity is not aligned with their gender assigned at birth. Some may allow the family to identify the person's gender and use only that to pick out gifts, business materials, and outfits to give. Others may utilize business or birth records and refuse to deviate. In either situation, items that are gender-normative (all pink for girls, all blue for boys) may not be a fit for many of the adults in your business, and this may be a conversation to have with the organization for overarching reasons, not just for employees who identify as a gender minority.

Safety Emergencies Occurring at Home

In addition to emergency situations within the business and difficult times at home, LGBT+ adults may become unsafe at home due to their sexual and/or gender identity. This may result in physical, emotional, psychological, or even sexual abuse. It may result in significant neglect of the person's basic needs. Sometimes this is rooted in a parent or guardian's anger about the situation. Sometimes it is a misguided attempt to change the staff member into something more acceptable to the parent or guardian. You may see physical damage or begin to see the employee's work begins to slip or their behavior change, or they may begin to attend business events or come into the office disheveled or appearing to be malnourished or unwashed. Unfortunately, not all homeless shelters or emergency centers is inclusive of LGBT+ people, so it is wise to know the options before recommending them to a colleague who appears to be in need.

The goal is simply to be prepared for an LGBT+ employee in need so that you are ready to act at the time the need arises, rather than trying to juggle the emergent situation and completing research to ensure their safety as you transfer or refer them to the care of others.

In Closing

It is important to hear and understand terminology from the perspective of those you are engaging in conversation with. Using a person's chosen term without judgment can make all the difference in the world. This means being open at all times, regardless of whether you understand why a staff member in your office has chosen to identify by a different name, gender, or a pronoun from those they have previously used in your office or in your business. The best course of action is to thank them for letting you know and then to use that name and pronoun when calling on them in meeting. If other employees question this, not every moment needs to be a reason to stop the meeting for a long lecture about these topics. It may simply be that you can say that this is the name this employee is using and then continue with your meeting. If you accept this information from the employee and behave as if it is no big deal, it is much more likely that the other employees in the meeting will behave as if it is no big deal as well. However, be mindful of what may be being whispered when you are at the front of the meeting or things that might be said in the hallway before or after meeting. You can always check in with an employee before or after meeting to ask if they are feeling safe and supported or to remind them that your office is a place where they will not be judged or mistreated.

Section II — Scenarios: Test Your Knowledge

Section summary

In this section, you will find scenarios that do happen, have happened, and are happening in businesses across America. For each, you will find a scenario situation, thought questions, and guidance.

How to use this section

This section can be utilized individually or collectively. If you are reading this on your own, read the scenario, take time to answer each question in your mind or on paper, and then turn the page to find out how your responses fit with the guidance by the expert, as if she were on-call to guide you through this. Then, you'll see suggested readings at the back of the book. This will allow you to imagine the potential results, receive guidance from the expert, and to find out what research indicates, or what peer-reviewed publications would be useful to buttress the situation if you were to present the scenario and the guidance to your business in order to create or update policies. If you are reading this as a group, the scenario can be read aloud and the questions answered collectively; or the scenarios can be assigned to different breakout groups for consideration, discussion, and sharing with the larger group.

Section take-away

The purpose of this section is to imagine and examine what would happen if the provided scenario situation occurred in your own business, and to become more thoughtful about the various ways of handling each situation.

Scenario I

A female employee in your meeting named Jessica has just come up to you before the start of an important business meeting and asked to speak with you privately. She discloses that she is transgender. She asks that you call her James and that you use male pronouns both privately and during the meeting. You have never had a transgender employee before and are uncertain how to proceed.

1. If you were the sole decision-maker at your business, how would you choose for your business to handle this situation?

2. Based on what you know of those in decision-making positions at your business, what decision do you think they would make about how you must handle this situation?

3. Utilizing only your business's employee handbook, what (if anything) do they dictate about how you must handle this situation?

4. If the answer to question #1 is different from the answers to question #2 and/or question #3, what can you do, in your role in the business? What (if anything) should you do?

SCENARIO 1.1

In addition to the information provided in Scenario 1, the employee discloses to you that their spouse knows about them being transgender, and they are "not at all okay with this." At the moment the employee makes this statement, other employees begin entering your office for the meeting. There is no time for further conversation with the employee without others overhearing.

1. If you were the sole decision-maker at your business, how would you choose for your business to handle this situation?

2. Based on what you know of those in decision-making positions at your business, what decision do you think they would make about how you must handle this situation?

3. Utilizing only your business's employee handbook, what (if anything) do they dictate about how you must handle this situation?

4. If the answer to question #1 is different from the answers to question #2 and/or question #3, what can you do, in your role in the business? What (if anything) should you do?

GUIDANCE

First, pat yourself on the back! This employee feels safe enough to share this with you, which means you are doing a great job modeling what it looks like when someone in the workplace is trustworthy. Next, get more information from this employee. Has James told others in the workplace? Will James be telling his colleagues directly or just letting them figure it out when he is called on in meeting by a different name? How does James want you to handle each of those situations if not everyone knows? Also, ask about James' emotions and consider his safety. Does James feel safe at business and at home? Have you noticed James' work quality slipping or him appearing to be struggling with anxiety or depression?

Now that you've gathered the facts, ask if he wants you to change all of your written records to reflect what James has told you. If he is not yet ready, tell him that you await his word and will act when he gives it. When he is ready, make sure that the documents you use for all Human Resources forms, for all name tags and security badges, etc. all say "James." This helps to ensure that James is called on appropriately. If you utilize computers or if anything is hung up in your office with employee names, change the name to James. This will allow James to continue to be in the office as himself, without having to log into a computer program using the name he does not use or seeing items on the wall with a name that is no longer his name.

When considering Scenario 1.1, this requires more information. Ask to see this employee after the meeting and ask if this means that he does not feel safe at home. If there is threat or experience of physical or emotional violence, proceed following the business's mandated protocol for staff member abuse. If you live in an area that is very anti-LGBT+ or promotes conversion camps, offer James the number of a suicide prevention hotline such as: The Gay, Lesbian, Bisexual and Transgender National Hotline, The Trans Lifeline, Trevor Project Lifeline or The GLBT National Youth Talkline (geared toward youth but their specific training in LGBT+ callers may still prove useful), The SAGE hotline (geared toward LGBT+ elders but also offering peer support, which may be helpful for adults of any age), or a national suicide prevention lifeline or crisis text line so he can gain support from professionals who are understanding and accepting of his identity. Continue to check in regularly with James.

Scenario 2

You are a leader who is well liked in your business. As such, you often hear gossip about employees in the business from the employees you most frequently interact with. You have just heard that one of your employees is gay. This employee participates in your office's department-wide sports team. This means that this employee will be changing out of business clothes and into other attire in the locker room with other employees of the same gender. You are not certain whether the employee's sexuality is widely known throughout the business. You are unsure how other employees feel about changing clothes in the locker room with someone who is attracted to the same gender.

1. If you were the sole decision-maker at your business, how would you choose for your business to handle this situation?

2. Based on what you know of those in decision-making positions at your business, what decision do you think they would make about how you must handle this situation?

3. Utilizing only your business's employee handbook, what (if anything) do they dictate about how you must handle this situation?

4. If the answer to question #1 is different from the answers to question #2 and/or question #3, what can you do, in your role in the business? What (if anything) should you do?

GUIDANCE

There are a lot of details in this scenario, so let's break this down into what we know for sure, removing all of the things that may be rumors, misunderstandings, or inaccuracies. When we pare this down, all we know for sure is that there are employees who think that one of your employees is gay. Before we consider anything else, the feelings of fear that others are uncomfortable with a person because they are gay indicates outdated beliefs that someone's sexuality inherently makes them less safe to be around. It also indicates that there may be a misperception that a person's being gay makes them deserve to be sexualized. It is important that you take time to consider this belief within yourself, both to change the mistaken thinking and so your inherent bias does not become foundational for employees.

In addition, when considering whether this bias may be existing for others, it is unknown whether the employee is gay, whether others are correct in their assumptions, and whether anyone cares. That is all separate from anything having to do with the locker room situation. With this in mind, your best bet is to simply check in with the employee in question. Since you do not know anything for sure about the employee's sexuality and they have not addressed it with you, a general check-in is your best approach. The intention is not to try to find out if the rumors are true or to get the employee to come out to you (if they are gay), but to ask how the employee is doing. Does the employee feel safe in the locker room? Are they being treated differently than their peers? Ask this in a space that is private enough for the employee to feel able to speak freely while being mindful of your business's policies on one-on-one conversations. (For example, many businesses require that employee–leader conversations occur in a place with a window or have the door open to prevent impropriety or the appearance of impropriety.)

If, after checking in with this employee, you feel that they may be struggling, follow the business's protocol for working with an employee who is struggling for any reason. This may involve including the guidance counselor, for example. Since this may be related to the employee's sexuality, talk with the guidance counselor or business social worker.

Now that we've got a plan for the employee, let's look at the locker room situation. We don't know right now whether there are any concerns by anyone about this specific employee. However, this is a good time to check policies and procedures about how this would be handled in the event that this scenario occurred, and it was a problem. If there is a plan in place, know what it is and consider, after reading this book, whether this is the most inclusive policy. If it is, awesome! We can move on! If not, find out who to discuss this with and how to work with them to create an improved policy that is inclusive. If there is no policy at all, ask the policymaker at your business if they would allow you to write that policy. If they will (or if they will allow you to write it with them), this would be a great time to create the most inclusive policy possible.

What might that look like? First, tie it into the existing anti-bullying policies. It is fairly standard that business policies state that bullying is not permitted for any reason at any time anywhere on business grounds or at business-related events. Thus, this would include locker room bullying. Next, consider the unique nature of an LGBT+ employee. Now, think about what other groups this may be true for. This could include people with disabilities, those with anxiety, employees with trauma due to abuse, and employees who may simply not feel confident in their bodies. Suddenly, this policy stops being "just about LGBT+ employees" and now becomes a policy about many employees. (This makes it tougher for the administration to refuse.) Perhaps your locker room allows for curtains or stalls to be installed, so employees have access to private changing areas. If not (or if there are not enough), is there a nearby restroom that employees can use for added privacy?

If this is for a sports team where a uniform is required, offering options for different changing areas, staggered start times so there are fewer employees changing at a time, or having a staff member within earshot of the locker room so that any bullying would be heard and interrupted could all work well to eliminate some of the problems with locker room anxiety and stress.

Scenario 3

It is time for a large quarterly company meeting in which many teams come together. you spot Mr. Johnson, one of the business's eldest and most beloved leaders. As you begin to approach him to say hello, you notice he is wearing pants, a blouse, and heels. When he turns around to greet you, you notice he is wearing lipstick. He notices your surprise and tells you that, since the last quarterly meeting, he came out to his family, and now he is "finally getting to be called Mrs. Johnson." You are unsure whether the company leadership or other staff members know about this.

1. If you were the sole decision-maker at your business, how would you choose for your business to handle this situation?

2. Based on what you know of those in decision-making positions at your business, what decision do you think they would make about how you must handle this situation?

3. Utilizing only your business's employee handbook, what (if anything) do they dictate about how you must handle this situation?

4. If the answer to question #1 is different from the answers to question #2 and/or question #3, what can you do, in your role in the business? What (if anything) should you do?

GUIDANCE

There are three things happening simultaneously here: your surprise, their happiness about their open identity as Mrs. Johnson, and you're wondering if others know about this. Let's start with that last one. Since you're coming into a meeting for all staff, whether others already know about this or are about to be surprised by this doesn't much matter, because soon the room will fill up and everyone will know. Since the lipstick and the introduction as Mrs. Johnson clued you in, they will likely do the same as others enter the room. So, there's no need to wonder, worry, or concern yourself with what others know. You don't even need to worry about you knowing what others do not, as Mrs. Johnson is not only choosing to wear a shade of lipstick that is obvious, but she is also openly talking about herself as Mrs. Johnson—and she is making a point of saying how happy she is about being Mrs. Johnson.

This just leaves your surprise and Mrs. Johnson's happiness about openly being Mrs. Johnson. While your surprise will dissipate as the new information becomes information you've known for longer and longer, what stands is Mrs. Johnson's happiness about openly being Mrs. Johnson. You can also presume that this new information may cause some comments and conversations from your peers. Mrs. Johnson isn't a fool; it is certain she knows this will probably happen, and she has likely spent days, weeks, months, or even years preparing herself for them. However, you do not need to leave her to brave that on her own. How supportive do you want to be right now?

You have three options. In order of least brave to most brave: stand or sit in the room in silence while the others in the room discuss this new information; stand or sit next to Mrs. Johnson and offer comments of support, knowing she is overhearing whatever may be being said about her; or roam the room, listening for others to talk about this and jumping in to either share words of support for Mrs. Johnson or shut down negative commentary.

While the bravest option may be tied to your seniority at the meeting or your knowledge and relationships with your peers, it also offers you the strongest opportunity to advocate and support someone who is in a vulnerable position in the room. Plus, since Mrs. Johnson has significant seniority, you would be buttressing on that while supporting her; if that does not feel like something that you can do, for whatever reason, sitting with Mrs. Johnson both to offer her words of support and to visually show solidarity can send a strong message to your peers about your beliefs concerning inclusion in businesses.

Let's say, though, that, at the moment, you weren't sure what to do so you just sat down for the meeting, saying nothing, and doing nothing regarding Mrs. Johnson. Now you're reading this, rethinking that moment, and wishing you would have done things differently. Whether that meeting was yesterday, last business year, or a decade ago, reach out to Mrs. Johnson now! Apologize to her for missing the opportunity to support her more directly. Ask her what you can do for her now to support her. If she has already retired, take time to think about and create a plan for the next Mrs. Johnson (whether this would be a staff member or an employee). Decide how you will show your support when that person comes out to the business as transgender. Then, when the moment happens, follow through. (You might even consider sending a letter to Mrs. Johnson to tell her how knowing her inspired you to act differently in the next situation.)

Scenario 4

On Friday after business hours, the federal government signed a bill into law that discriminates against LGBT+ people. You know that there are employees at your business who openly identify as LGBT+ and that there are employees who have LGBT+ loved ones. It is Monday morning, and you are commuting to the office. You know that the new law will be brought up at work by the staff, as it is considered to be major news.

1. If you were the sole decision-maker at your business, how would you choose for your business to handle this situation?

2. Based on what you know of those in decision-making positions at your business, what decision do you think they would make about how you must handle this situation?

3. Utilizing only your business's employee handbook, what (if anything) do they dictate about how you must handle this situation?

4. If the answer to question #1 is different from the answers to question #2 and/or question #3, what can you do, in your role in the business? What (if anything) should you do?

SCENARIO 4.1

How might this be different if the decision was made by your state's government?

SCENARIO 4.2

How might this be different if the decision was made by your local community's government?

GUIDANCE

This is a great opportunity for conversations about the way laws get made and how or whether the company gets involved in politics or encourages/discourages staff to be politically active.

For Scenario 4.1, continue the conversation but also offer the opportunity for your employees to find out about state-wide opportunities to speak with the politicians in your state. Encourage them to research the politicians making state-wide decisions and to find out how to be in contact with them to discuss their beliefs and how they want to encourage these state representatives to vote. This may include attending age- or issue-based lobby days, it may focus on attending town hall meetings when the politician is in their area, or it may be an opportunity for the employees to come together to work on requesting a visit by one or more politicians. Guiding them to do the research and to do the work not only helps them toward their goal but also encourages their activism and their sense of community as they work together to find ways to reach out to their own representatives. You may also want to discuss any workplace policies regarding posting political paraphernalia up in the office or taking time off from work to attend or participate in political events.

Scenario 4.2 can also be responded to in this way, though the local aspect may offer even more opportunity for employees to speak up about their concerns and their emotions. Some may have personal ties to one or more decision-maker. It may become easier to encourage one of the decision-makers to visit the business to speak with employees. It may be impactful for employees to write a letter individually or collectively to be published in the local newspaper. Television news may be interested in a story talking with employees as they speak out.

In addition, no matter which scenario is most accurate for the situation, be sure to offer employees continual workplace-appropriate opportunities to remain aware of situations before votes or changes occur so they can work to encourage what they believe or prevent voting on a particular issue from occurring, rather than to always being in a reactive role. This can be done in unison as a business, in concert with your colleagues, or as an ongoing topic within your own office. Talking with your colleagues may guide you in how to proceed.

Scenario 5

On your way out of business yesterday, you walked past an employee, Cameron, who was holding hands with another employee of the same gender. This surprised you, but you said nothing. This morning, the employee approached you. Cameron says, "So I know you saw me yesterday holding hands with Mickey. Please, please don't tell anyone. I don't think it would go over very well at the office!" Just as the employee finishes this sentence, another employee approaches you with a question about an upcoming work deadline. By the time you turn back to Cameron, they have walked away.

1. If you were the sole decision-maker at your business, how would you choose for your business to handle this situation?

2. Based on what you know of those in decision-making positions at your business, what decision do you think they would make about how you must handle this situation?

3. Utilizing only your business's employee handbook, what (if anything) do they dictate about how you must handle this situation?

4. If the answer to question #1 is different from the answers to question #2 and/or question #3, what can you do, in your role in the business? What (if anything) should you do?

SCENARIO 5.1

Would your answers to the questions change if Cameron were an intern? If so, how? If not, why not?

SCENARIO 5.2

Would your answers to the questions change if you were Cameron's boss? If so, how? If not, why not?

SCENARIO 5.3

Would your answers to the questions change if Cameron were your boss? If so, how? If not, why not?

GUIDANCE

Let Cameron know that you support them. If there are existing policies at work that protect their employment and protect them from bullying, offer to provide new copies via print-out or email of these for Cameron's reference. If there are no such policies, let Cameron know that you are working on creating such, as you have recognized this as a problem. Invite Cameron to assist you in this but assure them that, whether they help or not, you would never tell anyone about their private life.

In Scenarios 5.1 and 5.2, you must be mindful of the power dynamic. In both cases, Cameron is not only someone with a secret you now know, but they are also someone who may fear that this information will harm their written review or their chances of growing at the company. Assure them that you are supportive of them, that you would never disclose their personal information, and that this has no impact on how valuable they are to you in their professional role.

In Scenario 5.3, Cameron may be concerned about your sharing their secret or you're using the information in a way that undermines their authority over you and over others within the workplace. Assure Cameron that you would never share their personal details with anyone and that your respect for them has not changed due to this new information.

Scenario 6

As part of your business's mandated health insurance updated paperwork, you are provided with pamphlets given to you by the health insurance company meant to offer education to limit unhealthy practices that can lead to the need for medical treatments. You discover that the materials provided only include cisgender bodies and heterosexual relationships. While you do not know the sexual orientations and gender identities of every employee and staff member, you know that there are LGBT+ employees in the company.

1. If you were the sole decision-maker at your business, how would you choose for your business to handle this situation?

2. Based on what you know of those in decision-making positions at your business, what decision do you think they would make about how you must handle this situation?

3. Utilizing only your business's employee handbook, what (if anything) do they dictate about how you must handle this situation?

4. If the answer to question #1 is different from the answers to question #2 and/or question #3, what can you do, in your role in the business? What (if anything) should you do?

GUIDANCE

This scenario may seem, on its surface, as a no-win situation. It's easy to picture everyone wanting something different, and you and your business are stuck in the middle, right? It doesn't have to be that way! First, look at the existing materials used. Is it possible to request that the insurance company makes small additions to the materials to become more inclusive? For example, is it possible to turn a quiz about safe-sex behaviors into one without genders being used, swapping out "your partner" for gendered words? Is it possible for the company to create a statement or additional handout to provide to employees to articulate why gender and sexuality are being provided and to guide them toward recognizing inclusion and lack thereof as they read? This is likely the least disruptive method of correcting the problem.

You may also wish to discuss with employees whether the health insurance policy is as inclusive as the needs of all employees. This may be handled via conversation, through anonymous surveys, or through deciding that insurance plans must include same sex partners, gender affirmation care, and adoption options for same sex couples. Work with leadership to discuss what can be done and offer to create or join a team to research viable options if there is not an obvious option easily available.

Scenario 7

You are in your current role within your current business. One of your employees is openly gay. Recently, you assigned a group project, which is due in one week. The next day, you receive an email from one of the employees, Chris. "I am writing because of the group project you assigned. I would like to be put in another group. In our household, we do not condone homosexuality. As such, I do not want to work in this group with the homosexual employee. In addition, please ensure that I am never assigned to group or pairs work with this employee."

1. If you were the sole decision-maker at your business, how would you choose for your business to handle this situation?

2. Based on what you know of those in decision-making positions at your business, what decision do you think they would make about how you must handle this situation?

3. Utilizing only your business's employee handbook, what (if anything) do they dictate about how you must handle this situation?

4. If the answer to question #1 is different from the answers to question #2 and/or question #3, what can you do, in your role in the business? What (if anything) should you do?

SCENARIO 7.1

Would your answers to the questions be different if, instead of being openly gay, the employee was openly transgender? If so, how? If not, why not?

GUIDANCE

Depending on where you are, you may have already received an email like this, or you may not be able to imagine anyone receiving an email like this; American experiences vary so wildly depending on geographical locations and industries! However, since people relocate all the time, no matter how open your employee population typically is, a new employee in your workplace may come from a place where sending this type of email to you seems logical and right for their beliefs. When we remove all of the details, we come down to two options here: either reassign Chris to a different group and never put Chris and the gay employee together, or refuse to condone Chris' request and treat Chris, the gay employee, and all employees the same.

As a reader of this book, you've long figured out that the goal here is typically to enforce inclusion wherever possible and to remove stigma and ignorance. Chris would very likely benefit from interacting with many different types of people, as all employees do. We would also need to know whether the business policies, city policies, or state laws have mandates against discrimination against sexual orientation. If so, it would make sense to pull Chris aside and discuss the situation. First, hear Chris's thoughts and feelings on the subject. Listen to Chris' concerns, talk with Chris about the non-bullying policies that exist, let Chris know that his working with the gay employee is going to happen both now and likely on a periodic basis throughout his time with the company, and regularly check in with the group members individually and collectively to ensure a safe experience for everyone. This may also require you to include your supervisor, as sending a response to Chris' refusing to remove him from the group may create further tension or reaction by him. Your business may even wish to involve legal counsel simply to protect themselves.

In other businesses, it is preferred to avoid conflict thus moving Chris would be business protocol. Even then, it would be a great idea to speak with Chris. You'll also want to be sure not to cause the group members to take on additional work because of this, as it would not be right for an entire group to suffer due to Chris. For Scenario 7.1, the guidance would not change unless the business's policy specifically considers gender identity the same as gender for non-discrimination purposes. In this case, follow the same protocols as above, letting Chris know that you would not be legally permitted to make the requested changes.

Scenario 8

While walking from the cafeteria to your office, you overhear two employees calling a third employee names. As you approach, you hear that the names are based on the employee's sexual orientation. Before you get close enough to say something, the three employees see you and all run off in the other direction. Later, you see the third employee alone in the hall. You ask if everything is okay. They respond, "I know you saw the whole thing earlier, but it's nothing. I mean, it's not nothing, but it's no big deal. Just don't say anything, okay? Because if you say something, they'll think I said something and then it'll be way worse."

1. If you were the sole decision-maker at your business, how would you choose for your business to handle this situation?

2. Based on what you know of those in decision-making positions at your business, what decision do you think they would make about how you must handle this situation?

3. Utilizing only your business's employee handbook, what (if anything) do they dictate about how you must handle this situation?

4. If the answer to question #1 is different from the answers to question #2 and/or question #3, what can you do, in your role in the business? What (if anything) should you do?

SCENARIO 8.1

Would your answers to the questions be different if, instead of the comments being about the employee's sexual orientation, they were about the employee's gender identity? If so, how? If not, why not?

GUIDANCE

For every scenario in this section, you will need to take into account your business' non-bullying policies as well as any local, state, and federal laws that may protect against discrimination on the basis of sexual orientation and/or gender identity (or on gender in general). Although it is very common for victims of bullying to fear upsetting the bullies, you can point out to the employee that you witnessed the situation firsthand and that this will be stated to the bullies, to help make it clear how you became aware of the situation. In addition, while following the protocol for handling bullying situations, it may be a good idea to include the Human Resources or Legal department to ensure that the employee being bullied can be assessed for safety and offered resources.

Scenario 9

Your business is preparing for Community Night, an evening in which the business is open to the public, to meet the business staff, and to further community relationships. As such, everyone is hard at work beautifying the business offices. While walking down the hall, you realize that every poster promoting family support and togetherness depicts white families with a mother and a father. You know that there are members of the community in same-sex marriages and employees in the business who are of other races.

1. If you were the sole decision-maker at your business, how would you choose for your business to handle this situation?

2. Based on what you know of those in decision-making positions at your business, what decision do you think they would make about how you must handle this situation?

3. Utilizing only your business's employee handbook, what (if anything) do they dictate about how you must handle this situation?

4. If the answer to question #1 is different from the answers to question #2 and/or question #3, what can you do, in your role in the business? What (if anything) should you do?

5. If asked for feedback, what is an example of what you might say and who is the best person to have this conversation with?

GUIDANCE

First, yay for you for noticing something that has likely been going on all around you for years or even decades! You noticing this indicates a growth mindset that shows you are open to learning new ideas and that you are seeking ways to include all families and people in your business. We don't know how much time there is between this realization and Community Night to know if there is time or budget to purchase additional posters to add to the halls. If so, talking with the person who makes these purchases can be a great option to solve this problem. (Even if it's too late to receive new posters by this Community Night event, this conversation is a great one to have in order to prevent this concern for future Community Night events.)

What if there is no time to get new posters? How about involving interns or other leaders' helpers? A quick gathering of poster board and/or using the office computers can lead employees to create inclusive wall hangings quickly, and it lets them own the experience of thinking about how to make the space more inclusive to everyone who may come into their business. You can assign employees to support specific minority groups or types of families as you see a need, or you can task them to think about what types of people are not being honored or acknowledged on the walls and to create their own ideas from there. (Be sure to have them create a rough draft on scratch paper before using supplies to create the final posters so that you can ensure accurate and appropriate wording and inclusion!)

Scenario 10

Recently, your employee Jonathan has come out at business as transgender. Jonathan has now asked to be called Tiffany and to utilize female pronouns. During a staff meeting, a leader keeps talking about this employee, using male pronouns, and calling the employee "Jonathan." When you ask the leader about this, the leader rolls their eyes and says, "Oh, you mean, 'Tiffany'?" and uses air quotes.

1. If you were the sole decision-maker at your business, how would you choose for your business to handle this situation?

2. Based on what you know of those in decision-making positions at your business, what decision do you think they would make about how you must handle this situation?

3. Utilizing only your business's employee handbook, what (if anything) do they dictate about how you must handle this situation?

4. If the answer to question #1 is different from the answers to question #2 and/or question #3, what can you do, in your role in the business? What (if anything) should you do?

SCENARIO 10.1

Would your answers be different if the employee had reached out to complain to you about the leader refusing to use the employee's correct name and pronouns? If so, how? If not, why not?

GUIDANCE

Having made it this far through this book, it is understandable that this employee's behavior is giving you pause. (Yay for you for recognizing a problematic situation that may not have caught your attention before beginning this book! *high five*) However, we don't know what this staff member knows about gender or about transgender people, so we do not yet know whether this behavior is due to intentional misgendering and inappropriate behavior or someone who currently lacks the knowledge necessary to understand what it means to have a transgender person in the business and to understand appropriate responses to Tiffany both in her presence and out of her presence. Based on this, try to approach this employee privately. Explain that you weren't sure, based on their wording earlier, if they needed some support on the way to accepting Tiffany's name and gender pronouns.

(You can offer to share your copy of this book or recommend they purchase a copy. You can even offer to start a book club using this book and, later, other books on diversity.)

If the employee refuses or if the conversation with them indicates that they are aware yet intentionally misgendering Tiffany, speak with your supervisor. The goal is not to get someone in trouble; it is to protect Tiffany and other employees from being bullied by business staff. Before reporting this to your supervisor, you may first need to ascertain the supervisor's level of career and knowledge on gender and transgender people. You can offer the same guidance and support to them as you did to the employee. The goal is to help guide and educate folks so that Tiffany and others are treated with respect, both by those who have gained a career and knowledge base and by those who recognize that not treating employees appropriately will lead to career ramifications.

Regarding Scenario 10.1, this indicates an ongoing problem that has become consistent enough that the employee complained. While you will need to follow your business's protocol, you may wish to follow this situation more closely than more generalized complaints, as it may be necessary for business staff with training to advocate for the employee and for inclusive policies and procedures. This can help prevent those without understanding from creating repercussions or business protocols that can lead to unintended negative impacts on gender minorities within the business. You can also provide support to the individual while they are in business to ensure that they have a trusted colleague in the building.

Scenario 11

You are in charge of an office of employees, and you ask them to pair off to complete a training activity. As the employees separate into pairs, you notice that one employee, Jude, is being actively ignored by their peers. You decide to give the employees a moment to see if they self-correct, moving closer to listen in on what they are saying to one another. You hear them say that they won't partner with Jude because Jude is "weird." You do not know a lot about Jude, but you've been told by a leader in another office that Jude is "somewhere on the LGBT+ spectrum."

1. If you were the sole decision-maker at your business, how would you choose for your business to handle this situation?

2. Based on what you know of those in decision-making positions at your business, what decision do you think they would make about how you must handle this situation?

3. Utilizing only your business's employee handbook, what (if anything) do they dictate about how you must handle this situation?

4. If the answer to question #1 is different from the answers to question #2 and/or question #3, what can you do, in your role in the business? What (if anything) should you do?

GUIDANCE

Although the reasoning for Jude being ostracized is due to their being LGBT+, begin by treating this as you would any situation in which an employee is being left out. If those methods do not work, remind employees of the anti-bullying policies in your business. Make a point to check in with Jude before or after a future meeting to find out whether further intervention is needed.

Once the immediate situation has calmed, reconsider your process for partner and group work. Rather than instructing employees to create their own, do this for them. This prevents any employee from being left out or feeling anxious about being asked to work with their peer(s). You may choose to assign employees at random, you could choose to use groupings based on birth month or favorite ice cream flavor or another arbitrary detail that all employees would have an opinion on, or you may wish to partner or group employees in ways that seem arbitrary but that encourage teamwork and ensure that employees who may learn from another's traits consistently interact with that person.

Next, ascertain whether the comments about Jude were a momentary and passing situation that has been solved by redirecting the employees or if this is an ongoing concern. Rather than lecturing during the meeting (likely causing employees to blame Jude for this), intentionally incorporate as much diversity into the office as possible. This may be focused on LGBT + status, race, ethnicity, types of abilities, etc. and it may also be focused on all other types of differences and how differences are good for society and the industry you work within. For example, if you are dividing younger employees into groups based on their favorite ice cream flavor, take a moment to talk with younger employees about why it is good for the ice cream business that people like different flavors and how it is easier to share if people do not want the same thing at the same time, since it means no one gives up their favorite. If employees are older, encourage them to consider how diverse learners may interpret the assignment differently or how coming from a different culture may lead to different results in a group work setting. Your goal is not to divert from your intended lesson plans, but rather to be intentionally and mindfully encouraging employees to think about all of the ways diversity exists around them. This will allow them to begin to view differences, to see how these can lead to benefits, and to be more open to positively considering their own uniqueness as well as that of their colleagues.

Scenario 12

After being at your business for a number of years, you have become known for advocating for your company's business to support many local organizations and events. This ranges from sponsoring little league teams to 5k charity runs. One day during lunch, a handful of employees approach, asking if you would support their written request for the company to sponsor a community event. They tell you it requires no effort on your part; they will handle the details; they just need to write your name down on the application form for company approval and get you to sign it. You agree. When they hand you the form for your signature, you find out that the community event is the city's LGBT+ Pride parade event.

1. If you were the sole decision-maker at your business, how would you choose for your business to handle this situation?

2. Based on what you know of those in decision-making positions at your business, what decision do you think they would make about how you must handle this situation?

3. Utilizing only your business's employee handbook, what (if anything) do they dictate about how you must handle this situation?

4. If the answer to question #1 is different from the answers to question #2 and/or question #3, what can you do, in your role in the business? What (if anything) should you do?

GUIDANCE

Depending on your business, this may not even require any guidance! In many businesses, these organizational supports during Pride events have existed for many years without incident or concern. If your business is open to this group—and since you have read this book—you are a great fit for this, and it sounds like your employees are excited to lead the process, so just continue to support them the way you do all of the other groups you've supported!

If your business refuses the application to support a Pride evet, work with the business to find out their reasoning. Consider involving community leaders and the employee participants. You can also offer the business information about other businesses in the news who refused to allow this type of group and the ways in which it became problematic to refuse, as well as the ways in which businesses can gain customers and community goodwill by participating.

If the sponsorship is ultimately approved, be sure to incorporate mindfulness when discussing the situation outside of the group wanting to start this sponsorship. Not every employee participant may identify as LGBT+, and it may not be safe for some to be assumed to. In addition, it is never okay for anyone to out another person, so it is crucial to have ongoing conversations with employees about how to speak up for what they believe is right without making choices that jeopardize their own or someone else's safety or career.

Scenario 13

Each month, your business hosts a guest speaker. You are not sure who chooses the speaker or how the order is set; you simply know that you are tasked with being one of several staff members to sit in the auditorium and keep the employees quiet and seated during the presentation. At today's event, the guest speaker talks about the importance of family. As the person continues to talk, they begin to discuss the importance of having a mother and a father in the home. They stress that children growing up in homes without both mothers and fathers will grow up lacking life skills and they will always become a lesser-quality person than their peers. When they give examples, the speaker talks about how girls should be learning to cook and keep the house from their mothers and boys should be growing up learning to mow the lawn and fix the car from their fathers. You know that there are employees and staff in the auditorium whose homes include same-sex parents, single parents, and parents who teach non-traditional roles to their employees.

1. If you were the sole decision-maker at your business, how would you choose for your business to handle this situation?

2. Based on what you know of those in decision-making positions at your business, what decision do you think they would make about how you must handle this situation?

3. Utilizing only your business's employee handbook, what (if anything) do they dictate about how you must handle this situation?

4. If the answer to question #1 is different from the answers to question #2 and/or question #3, what can you do, in your role in the business? What (if anything) should you do?

GUIDANCE

This situation may make you feel the need for immediate intervention. Some readers may already be envisioning themselves yelling out from the darkened auditorium, arguing with the speaker, making a rousing speech about inclusion, and the speaker leaving in a disgrace while the employees all cheer for inclusion. A great closing scene for a movie, no question, but this is not really realistic. Instead, consider the ramifications of letting the speaker finish and then addressing the situation as a business. Maybe this means a business-wide announcement that acknowledges that families are absolutely important and that families can look very different to the ones described by the speaker but that they are all equally valuable. Maybe this means you find ways to incorporate the value of different types of families and people into your lesson plans or meeting discussion for the next several days, to challenge the idea that a family can only look one way. Speak with your supervisor to ascertain whether the business will be addressing this as a whole or whether you will need to speak to colleagues individually to share your concern and ask them to impart more inclusion in their offices to undo this narrow-mindedness on a smaller scale. Finally, talk with the business to find out who chooses speakers and how the speakers are vetted before being chosen. Find out about creating a checklist of requirements in order to approve a speaker. You may even ask to be on the committee choosing or verifying speakers in order to ensure this does not happen again.

Scenario 14

Like many businesses, yours now has regular active shooter practice drills. You are new to the business. Your role during these drills is to go to the cafeteria and guide the employees to a safe, less open space. This space has been designated to be the nearby bathrooms. As per the instructions, you are supposed to send the male employees into the men's bathroom and the female employees into the women's bathroom. Today is the first drill of this year, and it is the first time you have been assigned this role. During the drill, as you direct the employees, one employee points to another and says, "What about Dakota?" You remember that Dakota is transgender. While Dakota identifies as a woman, Dakota's business records have a male designation. In addition to making a decision very quickly for the purpose of this drill, you also want to make the right decision and make a great first impression on your new boss.

1. If you were the sole decision-maker at your business, how would you choose for your business to handle this situation?

2. Based on what you know of those in decision-making positions at your business, what decision do you think they would make about how you must handle this situation?

3. Utilizing only your business's employee handbook, what (if anything) do they dictate about how you must handle this situation?

4. If the answer to question #1 is different from the answers to question #2 and/or question #3, what can you do, in your role in the business? What (if anything) should you do?

GUIDANCE

In an active shooter drill or a drill related to any safety concern, the sole goal is to keep all employees safe. While it is understandable that you want to do a good job for your supervisor, this is not about you. It is about safety. That's it. As such, all that matters is that every employee is brought into a bathroom during the drill. Since many transgender employees experience bullying in the workplace, it is important also to maintain Dakota's safety during the time spent in the bathroom. Your goal is to make it safe for every employee to go into the bathroom that matches their gender identity. This means that Dakota should be instructed to go with the women into the women's bathroom. If there is not an affirming and supportive staff member going to each bathroom, but there is the option for you to choose which to go into to sit with employees, go into the bathroom with the transgender employee any time there is a transgender employee involved. This helps to ensure their safety during the drill in case there is any cause for concern. As a result, all employees will be in the bathroom, per your duties to move them into these locations, and Dakota and any other current or future transgender employee(s) will be kept safe during the drill itself.

Once the drill is over, speak with your instructor about whether there is an existing policy for these situations in regard to transgender employees. If not, ask to write it or to be part of the group that writes it. If there is a policy and it is not inclusive, ask to rewrite it or be part of the group that rewrites it. If the policy is inclusive, encourage the supervisor to make sure all staff are aware of the policy so that there is no confusion or mistakes made in the event of a future drill or true emergency. You may even wish to include this information where you keep your employee roster and any emergency drill instructions so that you and anyone who may be with you during this time have easy access to this.

Section III — Put Your Knowledge into Practice

Section summary

This section takes the foundational knowledge and the scenario hypotheticals and turns them into real-life action within your business(s). While it is understood that the readers of this book work within a wide variety of professional roles, the intentions for this section are to allow you to become more mindful of the realities of your spaces and the information being disseminated to your business's community so that you can make intentional decisions within the scope of your position to best support LGBT+ people.

How to use this section

Some chapters will apply to all, regardless of their role within the business. Others are specific to business subjects or job roles. You are encouraged to focus on the chapters most applicable to your own role, while also being mindful of the recommendations and guidance that benefits your colleagues, superiors, and those whom you supervise. While focusing on one's own scope of work is logical, understanding where there is opportunity to support others in areas outside of your particular role can allow for an overarching change within businesses, and it allows folks to support one another as they advocate for transformations within their own business roles.

Section take-away

This section offers the reader a way to assess their business's current inclusiveness, offers guidance on improving the physical space, policies, and protocols, and provides suggestions on office alterations to create a supportive and affirming environment.

Assessing Your Workplace

Although the previous sections may already have your mind swimming with ideas for change, before beginning to work to implement these ideas it is vital to become mindful of all of the areas in need of change. Some readers may be reading this book individually, while others may be reading it as a leaders' cohort, an entire business staff, an all-franchises or all-offices mandate, or an entire industry collective. Whatever your individual experience, you may wish to seek out a trusted colleague or suggest working together as a small group of people at your workplace location to assess your business, both so that there are a variety of opinions weighing in and so that there is already a contingent in place to begin the change process once the needs for change are fully recognized.

It can be easy to want to go back in time as far as possible when considering ways in which your business could improve upon its inclusion practices. However, this can result in significant frustration of wishing things would have been done differently when the focus now should be what can be done differently today and what can be set up so that situations occur differently moving forward. With this in mind, decide to consider the past one or two years and do not become distracted by what has occurred in the business before then, unless there's been a specific incident in your individual team or entire company's history. It is likely that your business has not changed its ways significantly in the past one or two years, so this allows for the consideration of continuity rather than focusing on something that may have occurred only once for a specific need for one person, one team, or one franchise or office location.

First Impressions

Although it can be easy to want to jump right into the business itself, begin by considering the experience of employees and their families. Pretend that you are brand new to the company. Obtain documents that would be provided to new employee. Think about what would be handed or emailed to them immediately upon their hiring, on their first day at the workplace, and at the end of any probationary period. Examine those documents carefully with the new inclusive knowledge you have. How many gender-marker boxes are on the form? Is there a place on the form for a staff member whose name is not the same as the name on their birth certificate? How are the spaces worded for anywhere where children's names and genders are listed (such as health insurance requirements)? When legal documents cannot be altered by the company (such as tax forms or insurance paperwork), is there a space on forms or an addendum option for gender inclusivity and to document the names the individual or individuals use, if these are not the same as on legal documentation? Are there any other areas on any of the forms that would indicate to an LGBT+ person that an employee who identifies as such is anything less than fully welcome?

Hiring Processes

Now, look into the hiring processes of your business or business district. First, begin by researching where a job opening is posted. This may be something you can access directly, or it may require you to reach out to the human resources department. If the information is listed only on the business or department's website, look at the website through the eyes of an LGBT+ person. Is there information on the website that indicates whether the business is inclusive? Is there wording on the website that only engages people who fall into the gender binary? Are there photos or drawings of business leaders or staff? Do those images depict different types and appearances of people? Now, review the job posting itself and other postings for other jobs. Are you seeing any wording that indicates whether or not the business or specific role is inclusive? Frequently, non-discrimination policies are listed either at the bottom of individual job posts or somewhere in the job board section of the website. Do you see that? If so, is the language fully inclusive, containing protections for individuals regardless of sexual orientation and gender identity? If the job is posted in places other than on the business's or district's website, where is it posted? If it is posted in public newspapers, websites, or magazines, take time to review those. Who is the audience for each? What are the images of people depicted in each? Does your community or city have a location-specific LGBT+ newspaper, magazine, or website? If so, does the business post job openings there with the same frequency they post them to non-LGBT+ specific places?

Next, examine the job application process itself. Some businesses still require handwritten documents. If yours does, request to review one from the human resources department. (They are typically standard for all positions within the business or business district, with additional department-specific paperwork required.) If the job application process is electronic, review this instead. As sexuality is typically not questioned or documented on the majority of job application paperwork, review the documents as if you were a person whose gender identity does not match the information on their legal documentation, such as a birth certificate or Social Security card, documents that are required to prove identity when being hired. On the application paperwork, is there a gender-marker question? If so, how many options are available? Is there a place for an applicant to document that they use a name that is not the same as the name on their legal documents? Is there a place to document that their diploma, leadership license, or work experience was awarded to or occurred under a different name? As you review these, also look to see whether the electronic process, if there is one, allows an applicant to continue to complete the paperwork if they leave a question blank. In some cases, for example, where the available gender options are binary, a person may feel they have no choice but to leave that question blank if neither of the two options are applicable. However, if the computer program does not allow the applicant to continue applying without answering that question, this is important to note.

Next, try to speak with someone in the hiring department to find out whether the business has any record of a transgender person or gender non-binary applying. Find out if the hiring department receives any training in the event of such an applicant and how they would handle it if the name on legal documents does not match the name on the application. In businesses where staff are assigned an email address that includes the person's name, find out if or how the human resources department would instruct the technology team to create an email address for a person whose legal name and the name they use do not match. Also, ask what the process is to change that email address in the event of a name change. It is likely that there is a procedure for this, as it is common for some married people to change or add to their last name. However, the information sought after here would be more aligned with the changing of a person's first name, as would occur in the event that a staff member began to use a different name that better aligned with their gender identity during the process of coming out and/or transitioning.

After Being Hired

Let's consider the experience for someone who has been enrolled in or hired at your company.

First, let's focus on the time between when someone is hired and when they begin their work at their desk or office. Does your business have any sort of orientation for new employees? These typically occur for new employees, though they may also occur for an employee who has transferred from one location to another. The intentions for these are typically to have the employees tour the business and interact with current employees who may be members of the company's leadership, the person's direct supervisor, and/or members of any team they may work on or colleagues they may be sitting near within the office space. Examine any flyers or emails that are sent out to alert the intended participants to these orientations. Is all language inclusive to allow all types of people to know that they are welcome? It is important to review these documents for inclusive wording and policies.

Now, let's consider staff training or orientations. Is there a process for training or introducing new staff? If so, what is this process? Does this have mandated paperwork to complete? In some businesses, this is where new staff would complete paperwork regarding health insurance, which may list family members' names. In other cases, staff may complete emergency contact forms. If your business requires either, review those documents. In some cases, health insurance paperwork may be mandated by an insurance company or by the federal government. In these situations, the documents may not be able to be altered to become more inclusive. However, there is nothing to stop a business from including a note in the paperwork packet to acknowledge that these forms are not fully inclusive and to articulate why the business is unable to alter them to make them such. While this does not change the form, it does allow the individual to recognize that the business is aware of the problematic language and that they do not support this wording. On the emergency contact forms, how are the options worded there? Is the assumption that a person would be listing their spouse or their parents? Many LGBT+ people have someone else who knows them best and would best represent their wishes in the event of an emergency. In addition, it is possible that some would prefer to include information regarding anyone they do not wish to have contacted, even if that person may be considered their legal next of kin. Is this an option on the existing paperwork?

Obtain a copy of the agenda for any of these orientations. If there is paperwork that exists to train the person who gives these orientations or if there is paperwork that the person in this role uses, examine those as well. Are these documents preparing to welcome all types of employees? If this occurs in groups, do any prior written speeches or scripts include phrases such as "ladies and gentlemen," which would not include people whose gender is non-binary? Are groups ever split based on gender?

During an orientation or introduction-to-colleagues experience for someone new to the staff, what information is pre-prepared? At some businesses, a name tag is already typed and waiting for each individual when they arrive. If your business offers this, where does the business get this name information from? While this can be problematic for someone who does not use the name on their legal documents, this not only impacts those whose gender identity does not match; it can also impact people who prefer a shortened version of their first name, who go by their middle name, or who may otherwise want to begin their collegial relationships using the name they identify with.

The Written Rules

Now that we have new employees hired and oriented, let's take a look at what the business has chosen to put in writing to address behavioral expectations.

Let's begin with the employee handbook. These are often sent to new employees and/or all employees in advance of the beginning of the business year. Review the non-discrimination policy. Look into the wording of any anti-bullying and anti-harassment policies. Are there specific policies related to sexual orientation and gender identity? If there are policies spelled out for bullying based on race, religion, or other groups typically associated with hate crimes, it is important to note whether sexuality and gender are also included. Are restroom policies listed? Is there anything in the policy dictating which employees may use which restroom?

Next, look at the dress-code section. It is very common for dress-code sections to be divided by gender. Is yours? Is anything in the dress-code policy discriminatory, based on what you have learned about gender identity and gender expression? For example, is hair length mandated for male employees? Are there any rules listed about makeup being for female employees only or about male employees being prohibited from wearing skirts or dresses? Smaller businesses and independently owned non-franchise businesses may be able to quickly make alterations. Larger businesses, corporations, and franchisees may need to speak with a larger governing body in order to request changes that are either specific to your location or to advocate for company-wide more inclusive changes to be made.

This should be considered carefully, and this part of the staff handbook should mandate how staff members are expected to respond when employees break a rule in the employee handbook. Is anything listed specifically on how to respond to an employee going through a gender transition? Is there anything specific listed on how to respond when an employee bullies or harasses a peer or a staff member for their sexual orientation or gender identity? Interactions with employee families may also be spelled out in this handbook. Is there anything listed regarding employees who are not accepting or affirming of an employee's sexual orientation or gender identity? This handbook may also list harassment policies between staff members. What is listed regarding the harassment of an employee based on their sexual orientation or gender identity? If this occurs, what do the handbooks say about how to report the situation and to whom? You may also want to find out if the person meant to receive that report has training that specifically includes sexual orientation and gender identity. Finally, this handbook may offer mandates or recommended guidance regarding how an office, office door, or other employee-facing space may be decorated. Are there any rules that would prohibit the inclusion of LGBT+ symbols or the symbols or acknowledgment of support of other minority groups?

Introduction into the Working Environment

Now that you've completed a cursory overview of the information that would be provided to new employees, as well as the handbook for staff, you can begin to consider the business experience itself. (If you are a business leader who works within more than one location or branch, you will want to do this for each building.)

(Remember intersectionality here and be mindful to examine this for all employees, including those who may have different needs, such as employees in wheelchairs, employees who are hard of hearing or deaf, and employees with developmental delays whose needs may be differently handled from those of the majority of employees. You may also need to assess private companies if your business outsources translators or technology accessibility programs for some employees.)

If possible, begin at the front doors of your business or wherever your employees enter the building each day, just as an employee would, envisioning the experience through their person's eyes. Walk through the halls and keep an eye open for anything that would indicate to them that this business is inclusive and accepting. You may find this in terms of inclusive stickers on front doors, office doors, or cubicle walls. You may find this in wording on posters or within the business information prominently displayed in the entryway, or by examining the way the business interacts with the community based on the artwork or informational posters hung throughout the business. Are the employees or community interactions depicted in posters and pamphlets throughout the business inclusive of individuals of different races, gender identities, and abilities? If they include depictions of families, do they show families that have same-gender parents or single parents, or families in which the guardians are connected to the kids in some obvious other way (such as grandparents with kids)? If there is information about showing romantic pairs, do you see same-sex couples? If there are pamphlets or other marketing materials about how families can benefit from your products or services, are same-sex couples included? Are the words used within these materials gender-neutral?

Assessing Your Business

Let's consider restrooms. If you were an employee at the business whose gender identity does not match the gender they were assigned at birth, would you know which restroom you would be permitted to use? If there are multiple restroom options for those with varying gender identities, how far are they located from where an employee may be in an office? Is it realistic to expect an employee to be able to move from the furthest possible office to that restroom and back, both without missing significant meeting time and without being uniquely impacted by traveling long distances each time restroom use is needed throughout the average workday for weeks, months, and years? Is this significantly different from the experience for employees whose gender assigned at birth aligns with their gender identity? Are there spaces in bathrooms for employees to have privacy? In meetings where employees are learning about any products or services that are used by couples or families, are different types of people depicted in the material? If so, are they depicted positively and equally to traditional family units?

In the Office and Collaborative Spaces

Beginning again with the employee's perspective, focus now on your space. Based on your role in the business, this location may vary widely from that of the average employee. For business leaders, this may be your office. For others, this may be the standard cubicle. For those who provide transportation, this may be the same vehicle each day or supplies you bring with you into each vehicle you use to transport employees. For other paraprofessionals, those whose work has them moving to the employees rather than having an office of their own, and those in the janitorial or kitchen staff, this space may be a supply cart, a section of a common area or computer lab; it may be your cafeteria line or your janitorial closet.

As you ascertain what areas or items to focus on for this section of the assessment, think about where you are most often found within the business. Consider where employees would find you if they were seeking you out and what you tend to be doing or carrying. The goal here is to become mindful of what message that space or item(s) may represent. Do you have any materials that show support of LGBT+ people? Are there areas where other beliefs or groups of people are shown? (This may be religious, it may be related to the clubs or groups your company sponsors, it may be in relation to the pioneers of the subject matter you focus on, it may be your personal hero, it may be family photographs at your desk, etc.)

Leadership and Learning Materials

In this section, since the focus of career is always on employees, it can be assumed that supporting LGBT+ inclusion in the workplace supports everyone within that workspace. As such, there is no need to differentiate here for the perspectives of every level and type of employee. (Thus, this may be the most cost-effective, efficient, and impactful way to insert LGBT+ inclusion.)

While the legalities of name changes and using the names employees request staff to call them varies by city and state, if your business allows you to call "Jaclyn," "Jacky," or "Jay" if they request, it is logical that your business (and/or you) ought to also support employees whose requested name is based in their gender identity. On a business attendance or time sheet or another place where employee information is documented for leadership how would an employee using a name different from their legal name be listed on the meeting roster? How is that name changed so that it appears correctly on all employee rosters and paperwork?

Looking at your specific leadership tools can seem specific to your subject matter or the role you have within the business. If your office has mandatory readings (including textbooks, conference materials, training, or supervisory worksheets, etc.), are LGBT+ people mentioned at all? Are there any areas in which LGBT+ people (real or as characters) are utilized? If so, are they depicted positively or negatively? For those whose job focus is administrative, consider your meetings on employee learning, employee enrichment, curriculum development, and all others that focus on how to better the employees' ongoing learning experience, as well as those that center on employment, staff retention, and continuing career/training for staff. Are there any that focus specifically on LGBT+ employees? Are there any that consider the needs of LGBT+ staff? How many focus on providing guidance for ways to include more LGBT+ awareness or diversity, equity, and inclusion? For those whose job focuses on employee and staff interaction while providing food, medical, janitorial, after-business, mentoring, or other services, do you receive any training for the specific needs of LGBT+ employees or staff?

In addition, some activities may already be divided into binary gender categories. This is most common in intermural sports. If your business participates in this and operates under one sports conference, you may not need to seek out information for each individual sport as the conference may have one manual that covers every sport within the conference. If this is the case at your business, you can review that manual, looking for any acknowledgment of LGBT+ people, as well as seeking out information about how a non-binary or transitioning employee would be permitted to participate.

How to Implement Change

Once you have gathered documentation that recognizes the areas in which your business community is already inclusive, as well as the areas in which there is minor or significant room for improvement, it is time to begin the process of creating and implementing those changes. For some readers, they may be in a position of enough power right this very moment to begin to draft these changes and submit them as new rules. For most readers, however, it may seem you are not in a position of power. As such, it can now feel as if you have become aware of problems but have no opportunity to solve them. Understandably, this can feel very frustrating. However, this does not have to be the case!

Now, you are likely looking at notes from information gathered during the assessment process and notes for how best to reach out to those in power positions to create and implement change. If this feels a bit overwhelming, that is okay! Certainly, if it were your job to make everything happen solely on your own, that would be very big job! However, this is very likely not the case. In fact, there may already be people who support creating a more inclusive and affirming environment. Maybe these are people who have also been required to read this book, if that is why you are reading it. Maybe these are people who employees have come to know they can trust and count on. Maybe these are other community leaders who frequently donate financially or in kind to various organizations and programs within your business. In addition, you may not know how many employees and/or their family members identify as LGBT + individuals and/or allies and supporters.

The first step is to take time to recognize who in your business system does have a level of power, either to directly influence or by being in a position to join you in your goal promoting consideration for increased inclusion. This may be an elder who is well respected, it may be someone known for championing new programs within the business, it may be founder, owner, or someone in a C-suite position, it may be someone on the business' board, or perhaps it is someone beloved by many regardless of their job title. Make a list of anyone who may be influential. Take time to think about the best way to approach each of these people. Some people may warm up best to casual conversation little bits at a time over a long period of time. Others may prefer a more formal sit-down meeting in which information is presented to them. Some may prefer to receive information or requests for support in writing via email. By best understanding how to approach the people you want to buy into making your business more inclusive, you increase your odds of gaining their support.

Since you are reading this book, talking about it can be a great way to initiate these conversations in a casual way. You can begin discussing something you have read each time you bump into a person whose support you are seeking. Maybe you can share a fact, or maybe you prefer to share a thought or opinion you have about some part of the book. This can be a great way for conversation to occur organically, both about the information within this book and as a bridge to have conversations about the thoughts and feelings this book has brought up in you. These can be used to ask about a person's thoughts and feelings in response or reaction to yours. For those you think would prefer a more formal approach, either verbally or in writing, the notes you have made while assessing your business can become a great place to begin the conversation. Keep in mind that while you have become significantly more aware of areas of concern in which improvement can occur, unless everyone is mandated to read this book at the same time you have been reading, you will likely be talking to many whose understanding and awareness of the needs of LGBT+ people may be at or below the level yours was the moment before you began this book. It is vital to be mindful of this so that you offer foundational knowledge to someone unaware without coming across to them as patronizing. If this is not something you feel prepared to provide, you can always refer back to this book for guidance. You can either utilize language from the book as it was provided to you, or you can share the idea that the person you are speaking with may benefit from taking time to read this book by talking about the ways in which you feel you have benefitted from this reading experience.

Sample Scripts

Here are some sample scripts you can use to reach out to individuals in writing (typically done via email or a business's messaging program) to schedule a meeting to speak with them regarding ideas you have for areas of inclusion improvement:

- I am reaching out to you after having read *Creating an LGBT+ Inclusive Workplace: The Practical Resource Guide for Business Leaders*. As I read this book, I began to examine the ways in which our business is successfully supporting LGBT+ employees, families, and staff. I have also found some ways in which I know we can do better. I would love to schedule a time to talk with you about both. Please let me know when you are available to meet.

- I wanted to reach out to you because I have begun to recognize that our business is not as LGBT+ inclusive and affirming as it could be. I know that, as a business, we pride ourselves in supporting the learning needs of all employees, and I would love to discuss ways we can be doing that better. When are you available to discuss this?

- As we gear up to begin another month/semester/year at BUSINESS NAME HERE, I have recognized that we have the opportunity to make some small but impactful changes that would support our business's LGBT+ employees, families, and staff. I would very much like to discuss these areas with you and to share ideas I have of how we can make these changes with minimal disruption to existing policies, procedures, and experiences for everyone. When do you have time to talk in the next week?

- I am curious as to whether you have had a chance to read *Creating an LGBT+ Inclusive Workplace: The Practical Resource Guide for Business Leaders* yet. I just completed it myself, and it highlighted for me where we are doing well affirming and supporting LGBT+ employees. I am so proud of us for those! It also helped me to recognize the areas in which we can improve. Let's schedule a time to discuss these!

In the Meantime/On Your Own

While the goal is to be offering information to those in power positions, to be collaborating with colleagues who already support making positive and more inclusive changes, and to be doing the work to get those changes in writing and approved, this can all take time. However, this does not mean you are stuck spinning your wheels! Instead, there are many ways in which you can promote LGBT+ inclusion and affirmation, regardless of your role in the business, regardless of your budget, and without making significant changes to the way you are already doing your job.

Physical Space

Whether your space is an office, cubicle, cart, supply closet, cafeteria, or other space, small changes may be overlooked by many but will be noticed by those most in need of your support. If you are allowed to use decorations in your space, include images of LGBT+ flags. (Remember that there are a variety of flags indicating support for different people under the LGBT+ umbrella. These include the generalized rainbow flag as well as flags specific to transgender people, agender people, lesbians, bisexuals, pansexuals, and asexuals.) Anywhere your name is listed or written, you can add your pronouns. Typically, they go after your name or under your name and in parentheses. For example:

Harvey Polis (he/him)

Marsha Rivera (she/her)

Gilbert Jones (they/them)

You can place this on your name tag on your staff mailbox, add it to your name on your door (if you have one), add it to any name tag or identification you wear while in the office, and anywhere your name is written.

If you supervise others, you may wish to begin this conversation by offering individuals the opportunity to give you information privately. To do this, consider offering a handout or sending an email as an opportunity to get to know your employees. The short form may include questions such as:

- How are you listed in the company directory? (Your full legal name.)

- What name do you want me to call you?

- What pronouns do you use? (Circle all that apply.)
  - She/her
  - He/him
  - They/them
  - Ze/Zim
  - Other: _____
- Where may I use these pronouns? (Circle all that apply.)
  - In meeting
  - With other business staff
  - In communication with your emergency contact

- Would you like to meet with me privately to talk about this? (Circle.)

  - Yes
  - No

- Is there anything else you would like me to know about your name or identity?

For those looking to simply share their own pronouns, they may choose in their email signature, they may be listed as part of a staff or business website where all employees have access to office information, or, for those in other types of work, if your business lists the cafeteria staff on the lunch menu handout and/or the janitorial staff on an office door or email, that is also a place where pronouns can be included. This does not cost any time or money and will likely be ignored by most people. However, those whose pronouns do not match the gender they were assigned at birth or the gender that correlates with their appearance will notice. This is an unspoken acknowledgment that it is safe for them to share their pronouns with you. In other cases, some may notice and inquire. This is an opportunity for you to explain that not everyone's pronouns match the gender they were assigned at birth or their appearance. By explaining this in a matter-of-fact tone, you provide information without judgment and offer them the space to ask additional questions. If you would like to be even more upfront about this, you can include this when you begin meetings and any time you introduce yourself by including your name and your pronouns. In gatherings with those whom you do not work with often, at the time that you would typically ask employees to let you know if you are mispronouncing their name or if they go by something else or ask them to go around the room and introduce themselves using their name and their pronouns. This may mean that you first need to explain what you are asking for and why. You should then set the example. You can give your name and pronouns to show them what this process is. (For example, "I will demonstrate by going first. I am Mr. Brooks, he/him" or "I will demonstrate, I am Mr. Brooks, I use he/him pronouns.")

Inclusive Curricula and Printed Training Materials

While many of us wish it were possible to either do away with current training manuals or industry standard protocols or swap them out for books filled with inclusivity and affirmation, this can be cost-prohibitive. In addition, as many businesses must utilize the same career materials for years or decades, a change to the materials would require significant amounts of work on the part of the business leaders as training programming, slides, and other documents would all need to change in order to support and supplement these materials. This can be unrealistic for many businesses, and it can put an undue burden on business leaders who are already frequently overworked. As such, until the time when your business is considering or planning to replace/update their materials anyway (at which time advocating for inclusive materials is vital), it is important to discern how to take existing materials and texts and make them more inclusive. The goal is inclusivity, but the secondary goals are to make changes that require little to no time, effort, or supplies. This makes the change as seamless as possible without adding stress onto business leaders.

In Closing

There has long been a saying, "Nice guys finish last." Typically, it is intended to mean that the only way to get ahead in life is to not be so nice. However, the reason others often finish first is not that they are not nice or unkind or even ruthless but because they have the support of others. If you pause for a moment to think about it, it is likely that you'll be able to think of people in most any industry who gained seniority due to nepotism. You can also likely think of others who succeeded because they had mentors who guided them, wrote letters of recommendation for them, were professional references, or offered to introduce them to someone who was in a position to offer them work or other valuable professional information. It is incredibly likely that most or all of the examples you've known were white and male. It is likely that all of the examples you thought of were heterosexual and cisgender.

"Old boys clubs" are not a new concept. Many movies have depicted scenes of them within various professional industries. Often, they are shown at golf courses, in smoking rooms, over drinks in bars, or on vacations together. Although these appear to be social in nature, they are often also how friendships and partnerships are founded and reaffirmed. As a result, those who are invited to participate in these experiences are more likely to succeed than others. For decades, women have been working to succeed in spite of being kept from these bonding rituals. After many years, social clubs, and networking events specifically for women are becoming more common. It is most common for these groups to be primarily heterosexual and cisgender. However, most leaders of most companies remain white, male, cisgender, and heterosexual. What about LGBT+ people?

In addition to often living in states and cities where an LGBT+ person can be mistreated with microaggressions for being LGBT+, these individuals are also fighting for the opportunity to succeed professionally, just like everyone. However, LGBT+ people are too often kept out of conversations, resulting in fewer opportunities to succeed not because of their talents or abilities but because of their lack of access to the same elite that others can access due to their backgrounds or upbringing or because a straight cisgender leader sees themselves in a subordinate. In some cases, LGBT+ employees, especially those who also identify as women, experience finding themselves on a "glass cliff." (This is the term created by Michelle K. Ryan and Alexander Haslam that acknowledges the occurrence of when a failing or struggling business promotes a woman or an LGBT+ person into a leadership role during times of significant stress.) This is problematic because it sets the individual up for failure. Some may wonder why the person would take this job. Unfortunately, many may only get this type of opportunity to lead. In other cases, a person may not know about the business' situation because that insider information was not shared outside of the boys' club they do not fit into. In either case, the person entering the role is at a higher chance of failure, not because they are not qualified or capable but because the system and the support around that role is floundering. Much like the well-known often discussed glass ceiling, this situation highlights the inequities faced by members of marginalized communities within the business world.

However, it does not have to be this way. Employees can work to support their leadership rather than to contribute to the person's struggle. C-suite leaders can be intentional not just in how the company hires its LGBT+ employees but also how the individuals are trained, mentored, and guided toward professional success. Every staff member regardless of their seniority can be active in their allyship in the workplace, helping to reduce or eliminate workplace bullying, harassment, and discrimination.

In a world where "nice guys finish last," it is incumbent upon every current and future business leader to consider whether their own actions or inactions are causing some members of their team to struggle, to be more easily ignored, or to be less often positioned for success. After reading this book, it is the author's hope that you consistently revisit these insights, consider your privileges, identify your allyship opportunities, become more aware of your newly opened mind, and recognize your position within your industry. With these insights, may you take every opportunity to better support LGBT+ people in your professional community, from the hiring process to the employee's success in your industry and excel in your field as a leader to all, not just to some.

Appendix I: Opposition

Although this book is intended to be useful, guiding, and inspiring, it would be unwise to pretend there is no chance of opposition in response to the goals and efforts of making spaces and office materials more LGBT+ inclusive. By recognizing this as possible, we can better prepare for the situation if and when it occurs. This allows for a calm and intentional response, rather than an off-the-cuff remark or statement made in anger which could become more combative than helpful in moving equality forward within your business.

Let's take a look at the stakeholders, where their opposition may stem from, and how to respond to it.

Business District Leaders (including C-suite and Board Members)

Depending on the area, those in powerful positions may have little or no direct involvement with your business' employees. They may also spend their time managing political expectations and aspirations, writing policies and procedures, and/or otherwise basing their work on many aspects of business that are not necessarily aligned with the realities of in-business experiences and needs. This is typically not an intentional disconnect, but rather an unfortunate byproduct of overworked individuals trying to juggle a variety of responsibilities and decisions without enough time to regularly engage with those who work in the businesses.

If opposition happens here, begin from a place of offering guidance. Perhaps the concern is that making room for LGBT+ inclusion means undermining the current goings-on of the business. Perhaps the concern is that adding LGBT+ inclusion means lessening the focus on areas where sales or other numbers requires high employee scores in order to continue to receive funding or to meet specific goals mandated to them either by a franchise board or by previously set annual or quarterly expectations. Before responding to the complaint, clarify what the person is afraid of. This will allow you to respond to their anxieties. It may be helpful to recommend a copy of this book to offer them the foundational knowledge that may provide them with enough understanding to recognize the importance of LGBT+ inclusion in businesses. It may be helpful to offer them the most recent studies on LGBT+ adults bullying and suicidality. It may also be helpful to offer to show them ways in which you are incorporating LGBT+ inclusion and affirmation into your office or business building without it costing time or money. This way, either you can end their apprehension, or you can know that the stress comes not from a lack of knowledge but from a difference of opinion and priorities.

While there is not always a way to convince top leaders to understand and appreciate the ways in which adding in conversations about diversity, equity, and inclusion benefits employees, by framing the focus on the benefits of employee mental health, by tying it to the most recent studies on bullying and suicidality, and by showing how the addition does not take away from business goals, you are most likely to at least calm them enough to avoid opposition that attempts to remove LGBT+ inclusion from the business. Over time, as they see that budgets and work productivity do not change, they may become less interested in whether or not LGBT+ inclusion occurs. Over more time, as they see that, in addition to no negativity, mental health improves or the suicidality rates in the business do not increase, they may even come on board to support the inclusive changes.

Business Leaders (including Supervisors and Department Heads)

Commonly, people in these roles have to walk a line between supporting their business employees and answering to their supervisors. This can place them in precarious positions, especially when a business is working to make changes that can cause waves to start within both groups of people. Often, if their supervisors are supportive of LGBT+ programming, business leaders will get on board, if only because they do not feel it appropriate to second-guess or argue with their bosses. In some cases, when many business employees are supportive of LGBT+ programming, the leaders can ascertain that this offers enough vocal support of the change that it can lead the district leaders to become more open to ideas or more supportive of them. By understanding which side is struggling with this planned change, a person can better assess the hesitation in the business leader(s) at their own business.

In some cases, business leaders struggle with the responsibility of overseeing the numerous changes within their business' building. If this is the case, offer to assist. This may be by looking into more inclusive images for the business' walls and website. This may be rooted in working with colleagues to review and amend lesson plans. This may be in offering ongoing support to the business leader through the change process or through offering ongoing auditing and revision of LGBT+ inclusion at regular intervals throughout one or more business years. Find out where the frustration or dread is coming from and do what you are capable of to tackle tasks or provide support.

Company Employees

Often, opposition from business employees occurs when it appears that new programs or policies will result in an increased workload to those who are already overworked. It can be easy for them to envision being forced to rewrite every training manual, to redo every office, and to change every way in which they have been working for the number of years they have been contributing to the success of employees in your business. This opposition happens frequently because increased workload often occurs. As such, it is no wonder that some in your business may have an immediate negative reaction to word that LGBT+ inclusion is beginning! Luckily, though, this can be an easy problem to overcome.

First, recommend this book so that they can utilize the same foundational knowledge that you now have. This can help them to understand why LGBT+ inclusion matters. Next, guide them to see how little has to change from their current practices. For example, asking employees their pronouns costs no money and takes only a moment longer during a meeting where people are sharing their names before the meeting begins. Offer to take time to walk through some of their current practices with them to provide guidance on how to incorporate more LGBT+ figures and topics without making any significant changes to the plans and materials that have worked well for them and that have been well received by their employees. You can even refer them to the section in this book that fits their focus area, where they can do a quick read to gather ideas. This can help get them thinking while also reinforcing that no one is expecting them to scrap everything and start over. This ought to lessen the anxieties and stress that many may have felt when they found out there were changes coming to the business, without having recognized the minimal amount of effort it would require of them to make those changes in their work.

The other common reason for opposition from staff is one of an argument that LGBT+ people/behaviors/issues go against their personal beliefs. This may be stated as being religiously based, and it may come from the way they were raised; it may be rooted in their culture. While the goal is never to make a person feel uncomfortable in the workplace, it is vital that businesses be mindful of inclusion and equal treatment for all, regardless of the personal beliefs of their staff. It may be helpful for those with these concerns to utilize the internet to search for support or career groups for LGBT+ people who share the same religion, background, or culture. This may help to show them that these traits and an LGBT+ identity can exist concurrently. It may be useful to recommend the staff member learn about the changes being made so that they see that the business is promoting inclusion and acceptance, just the way the business promotes this for people of all religions, backgrounds, and cultures.

Often, employees who speak openly in opposition are either repeating what they hear at home or via the media or are trying to sound tough in front of their peers. If an employee speaks up in defiance of LGBT+ inclusive learning material, the change of someone's pronouns, or in any other way, handle the situation publicly and privately. Publicly, address the employee in the moment of their behavior, just as you would for any other insubordination. Depending on what occurs and the commonality of the employee's behavior, this may be a verbal reprimand or refocusing, it may be to remove them from the office, or it may be to give a punishment. This allows all employees to see that you will never tolerate this behavior.

It must also be considered that the employee may be struggling with their own identity or parroting what they hear elsewhere, so it is also important to give the employee the opportunity to explain themselves privately. Ask the employee to stay after meeting and then ask them to explain their comment or action. Their response may warrant a referral to the human resources department. They may also simply need guidance that these comments do not impress you or their peers and that the repercussions will become increasingly severe if the behavior does not stop. The goal is to provide career and empathy.

If the staff member refuses to comply or if you find they have begun to undermine the business becoming more LGBT+ inclusive, it is important to document the situation and to bring it to the attention of their supervisor. It does not benefit anyone when an employee is working against the collective goal and it can be detrimental to the mental health and to the physical safety of LGBT+ employees and thus cannot be tolerated. If the staff member is open to learning, shadowing a senior or leadership employee may be beneficial as part of a training or probationary process. If they are not interested in this or if this is not guiding them to become more on-board with the changes to promote LGBT+ inclusion, they may be a better fit for a role that does not interact with other employees or perhaps they would be happier working elsewhere.

Employees' Families (including Spouses/Partners, Children, and Other Loved Ones)

Since most employees share their lives with loved ones, the opinions of those outside of your workplace can impact how your employee feels about inclusive changes within the workplace. Many families have limited information regarding LGBT+ people. Their knowledge base may come from the myths and stereotypes they have heard in their own upbringing or from whatever media or news they choose to watch. This can result in substantial fears. While it can be easy for folks to assume that the negative response comes from someone who is stupid or horrible, the reality is that most families are simply trying to advocate for the safety and success of their own employees. Begin by responding to the opposition by assuming good intentions. Offer information about the reason why you are making the choices that they are fighting against.

This may occur by providing statistics of LGBT+ adults suicidality and discussing the business's efforts to combat all suicidality by offering the inclusion of various minority groups and via anti-bullying policies. This may come from providing information that talking about sexuality and gender does not actually make a staff member become gay or transgender. It may be necessary to confront the idea that a staff member interacting with an LGBT+ person is not suddenly going to become infected with HIV/AIDS. So often, people's misunderstandings lead them to a place of fear. By calmly providing career in a way that is not demeaning, you may end the opposition simply through offering the science and research both to end the misunderstanding and by showing how many different minority groups are discussed and honored throughout the office and business, as well as majority groups.

If this does not work, it is incumbent on the business leader to work with their supervisor to handle the matter just as is done every time an employee complains about something that will not be changed due to that employee's complaint. While so many families want to have control over what and how their employee learns, businesses frequently have to let folks know that their feedback is heard but not going to change how things are done. Whatever tactics are used in all other situations of such requests or demands, they can work here too.

Appendix II: Interviews

Section summary

In this section, you will read exclusive interviews from some of the world's leading experts. They span a variety of age ranges, identities, locations, and industries. They share their personal stories in becoming top-level leaders, as well as insights into the past, present, and future of their industries' inclusive practices and beliefs. Finally, they'll share with you some of their best advice for how to get ahead and become as successful as they are!

How to use this section

This section can be utilized individually or collectively. Whether you are reading this on your own, as a small group, or in a larger training, you may choose to seek out people who are similar to you demographically. You may wish to focus on those in industries of interest. Perhaps you decide to read them all and compare the similarities and differences. It is truly up to you!

Section take-away

The purpose of this section is to imagine and examine the leaders' stories, insights, and advice and consider how to best apply it to your own professional goals and aspirations.

Lau Viggo Albjerg

Independent Career Coach and Management Consultant
white, cisgender man (he/him), gay

> Lau Viggo Albjerg is a leading independent career coach and management consultant
> with international experience and knowledge. He has worked with GlaxoSmithKline
> and Colgate-Palmolive as a brand manager, as well as currently working as a business
> owner, managing the careers and personal brands of many of the world's future
> leaders.

Please share your story

My career path was a bit untraditional as I did not find my place in the
world until I had spent some time traveling and getting to know myself. I
had traveled to Australia when I was 24, I had been working prior to that
as a photographer, then as a flight attendant, but it was never what felt like
what I was supposed to do. I took six months in Australia working there
and it turned my life around. Before that, I had felt a sense of shame about
my sexuality; I felt cool to not be a part of the gay environment; I was gay,
but I did not want to be perceived as a part of that lifestyle. Then I went to
Australia. It was a whole new world where there was such an ease with
who people were. I worked at a cocktail bar and blossomed in terms of my
confidence in my sexuality! I really realized how important it was for me to
feel and to be honest and authentic. It led me to realize that the gay
community was so important because we had to create safe places to be
ourselves and to feel confident and, well, normal, in our society.

Then I came back home and all I could think of was how to get out
again, to explore more about myself, my sexuality, and the world. I got
accepted to Business Law School, but my focus was about how could finish
my education and get out in the world as fast as possible. I declined business
law and enrolled for a 2-year diploma in marketing economy. For many
years this was always a feeling of regret. Most of my friends and colleagues
all have master's degrees and later in my career, when I started to work for
the big corporations, I always felt disadvantaged in comparison to my peers.
It played to the feeling of being the odd one out, the one not as good as the
rest. I felt like I did not belong in yet another way. In many ways, the
education I got was heavily influenced by my sexuality. Business law or
Marketing ... two very different things and in all honestly completely
random choices. I didn't know what I wanted to do. My head space was
filled with thoughts about finding confidence in my identity and belonging
somewhere. During this time, I wished I had had a support system, from
likeminded peers, who could help me navigate during this confusing and

defining time. It caused me to lose some focus on my own career management. This is a big reason for why I am doing what I am doing today.

Over time, I networked my way into many incredible positions at international corporations including one at GlaxoSmithKlein. I later moved to London to work with Colgate. I worked in marketing and had some great positions with a wide responsibility. But as I grew older, I also noticed I started to lose my passion for my work. In the end I realized that there was no way out other than leaving my corporate career and taking some time out to explore what I was truly passionate about. Through my career I also had these "what if" thoughts. One of those was "what if I had gotten a master's degree?". I had told myself for so many years that this was really the reason why I didn't feel confident in my work. Today I know if wasn't but deciding to go back to uni and finally obtaining that master's degree has been a significant personal achievement.

Since leaving a corporate career, I have trained as a coach, worked with career transition, and are not using my own experience from the corporate industry to help others navigate in their career management. Because I found out that my passion, what gives me energy, was actually helping others to build professional lives that feel fulfilling for them and sharing the knowledge and experience I has learned myself.

In summary, I guide people to listen to themselves, to become clearer and more authentic, so they can build careers they love while getting stronger in loving themselves too. That said, no matter what I do, I am always learning about myself too, which are life lessons I also translate into finding new ways to keep helping others!

What do you remember about your early experiences or considerations for LGBT+ people in your industry?

I think a lot of big companies had a general perception, but they see it as not actively harming LGBT+ people but not specially caring for the group either. Much like "all lives matter," Their intention was well-intentioned but not specifically focused on caring and enhancing that aspect of their employees.

However, some corporations have gotten this very wrong! A friend in my field once worked for a company where his department had an actual gay award, which was given out at the annual holiday party. It was seen as a joke; if someone wore colorful socks, it was assumed as "that's so gay" and that made the person eligible for a nomination for the gay award. It was shocking for me how they had no concept of how wrong this was. My friend had to be the one to stand up and speak up and this only happened after some time, and in the end, my friend left that company. I think this is a great example of a heteronormative non-diverse culture that created an island mentality. It's like the fairy tale of the emperor's new clothes but without anyone shouting the emperor wasn't wearing any clothes. In a culture with a diverse and inclusive ambition, this would never have happened, someone would have prevented this before it began or immediately upon the inventor trying to add this to the company's culture.

What have you seen change since then?

Many companies are working to improve. Colgate is a great example. On World AIDS Day, they send a company-wide email with information, educating everyone, and they offer help and support for those who need medication or testing. I know this did not always happen. It made me so proud to see them using their power to plant some information with their employees. For me, it was them owning their diverse employees and making a taboo subject be more openly discussed. It wasn't in a way to promote themselves externally, it was just an internal email.

However, this varies a lot depending on the industries. I find that the corporations with female or diverse leadership typically have more empathy.

Where do you think your industry or company will go next in terms of LGBT+ inclusion?

I think it's going to be interesting. It is showing that this is becoming top of mind more frequently. Some companies are trying to engage in this in truly inclusive ways. Other companies claim to create and celebrate diversity programming or goals, but the entire leadership team has no diversity whatsoever. That speaks volumes.

The younger generations are much more aware of what companies need to do to truly own LGBT+ inclusion in the workplace. I hope this will lead to more changes. However, it has to start with management, who must see the value in doing this work. There are some great examples of it working well as well as marketing mistakes that harm corporations. Every time this happens, everyone learns. Every time a mistake happens, it becomes clear that not having a diverse decision-making group costs the brand value of the company. Every time an inclusive advertisement is well-received, it shows that this can happen without problem and that it can become a viral way that inclusion drives and increases business.

What guidance would you give to other current/future business leaders about why being LGBT+ inclusive matters?

You truly must engage with these groups. Recognize that you are at a disadvantage that you do not automatically know the experiences of this group. Listen to members of the community and be willing to learn, to be wrong, to become better, and to keep doing this. You need to recognize that you not only need to say that you believe in diversity, but you also have to act with this in mind. You have to mirror society and society has to see themselves in your company. However much you want to say you believe, if your actions do not show it, your concepts are not going to be successful.

For those who can, travel! Choose to visit places very different than what you are familiar with, very different from your own life experiences. Stay there for a while. Whether you are going to another country or another city, choose a place where you are in a minority. Experience what it feels like to be judged, mistrusted, and questioned. Feel out being the "odd one out" can give you perspective in ways you cannot get from reading a book or trying to imagine what it must be like.

Hold yourself accountable. This is not something you spend time with once in your lifetime and never again. You have to keep learning and growing. Sometimes people mistakenly think that what was once okay suddenly became not okay, whether this is related to the terms we use to refer to someone or the images we use of a population or slogans or assumptions. However, it was never okay, people just did not have the ability to say this without significant repercussions. It was always hurting them, and they just put their heads down. To speak up now is not someone changing the rules, it's finally feeling safe or empowered enough to say what they have always felt and always known. It is not up to the majority to say what is offensive and hurtful, it is up to them to listen and to do better when you are told. To do otherwise is prejudicial, privileged, and intentionally harmful. To be an effective leader, you have to always be willing to put the needs of those you are leading ahead of your own and do everything you can to be inclusive and supportive so everyone can be their best selves in their workplace. It is not a choice, you must.

Lauren Banyar Reich

Founder of LBR PR
white, cisgender woman (she/her), heterosexual

Lauren Banyar Reich is the founder of LBR PR, a boutique public relations agency that combines high-touch service and impactful results with a transparency and authenticity that is unique to the PR world. With this distinctive approach to public relations and strategic communications, Lauren has helped her clients heighten brand awareness, increase donations, drive website traffic, grow market share, sell products and services, and develop thought leadership platforms. Her expertise spans positioning, traditional publicity, social media planning and execution, content strategy and development, influencer outreach, celebrity endorsements, partnerships, product launches, managing event logistics and booking speaking opportunities.

Lauren previously managed the agency day-to-day as Vice President and Director of Janine Gordon Associates (which was acquired by Peppercomm). She then served as the lead luxury specialist within the agency's consumer group, JGA Peppercomm. Lauren also spent four years at Jane Wesman Public Relations, a respected book publicity agency, and began her career wrangling celebrity talent and managing production for major fundraising events.

Throughout all of her work, she is known for using her unique skillset to find the best in her clients and to guide them to becoming known for being the best in their industry!

Please share your story

I made two very good decisions when I was 18 years old; one was choosing my husband and the other was choosing public relations and communications as my major. I hate that you have to declare a major at that young age, but I was looking to my teachers and advisers and they were really complimentary about my abilities to communicate and be persuasive and they appreciated my writing. They led me in this direction, and I went with their expertise and guidance. I went to University of Maryland College Par's Journalism School due to it being one of the top 3 programs in the country. It was incredibly challenging! However, I loved it because I learned so much from my professors. I always wanted to move to NYC after college, but I graduated post-9/11 so there wasn't a ton of opportunity there. In 2004 my then boyfriend (now husband) and finally made the plunge and moved to New York city. There, I landed a job working with a small but respected boutique book publicity agency where I worked with best-selling authors and subject matter experts. It was a constant influx of information and I never got bored. There was always something new to learn and promote!

As I grew in that role, I really began to understand the strategy and business behind PR and the value we provided for our clients.

Soon, I realized I wanted more responsibility and to manage others. In my next role I oversaw a talented team of publicists. I was able to still do the work, but also lead the strategy and most importantly, manage a team – advocating for those who worked under me and helping to mentor them in their careers. We did so well as an agency that we were acquired by a large firm. Unfortunately, this put layers between myself and the client, which removed so much of the relationship building that I had adored, so ultimately, we parted ways and I decided to start my own firm.

Being an entrepreneur can be really challenging because YOU are where the buck stops, but it also allows me to make decisions about the clients I work with and the employees I want to surround myself with. I had built a reputation of being someone who worked well with difficult clients, but this meant I was often given the difficult clients, which was a great skill but not something I wanted to deal with every day! Being able to choose this and having a "no jerks" policy makes my business stronger and makes the workplace so much better for me and for my employees. Value alignment between our clients and our company is becoming increasingly important, especially as we continue to grow.

What do you remember about your early experiences or considerations for LGBT+ people in your industry?

When it came to visibility, all the way back to when the movie moguls had a stable of manufactured stars, this was always something that would never be talked about. It was always kept very under wraps. Whether it was spoken or not, everyone knew that even the potential that someone was LGBT+ meant they would likely be shunned. Of course, social media didn't exist, so it was more about squashing rumors by having fake romances or the like occur. Things changed significantly when paparazzi and social media began to take hold!

What have you seen change since then?

I think one of the most interesting changes in the media is that it is now okay to not just be one thing. When I do this work, it is now about showcasing multiple versions and sides of the same person. Now you can be a couple of things, a mom AND a business owner or a woman *and* a CEO, etc. It makes any one thing less defining because you can be multiple things. We no longer have to hide or dismiss differences; it is now becoming okay and people want to know more about people who are visible—whether it's a celebrity or business leader. Social media highlights this desire for transparency and insight into who a whole person is, not just one aspect of them.

Now, being LGBT+ is not only not something we have to hide, but it can also be seen as a point of difference when marketing an individual, a company or product and services.

Where do you think your industry or company will go next in terms of LGBT+ inclusion?

When I think about inclusion in the future, I think about how problematic it is right now is that brands are inauthentically utilizing their position on marginalized communities as a way to market. I think people are going to keep calling this out and, over time, companies are going to have to be intentional about following through. For example, they won't be able to slap a rainbow on a product to pick up that sale but also fund politicians who are anti-LGBT+. I think it's going to become crucial that every brand is authentic and that they really walk the walk. This means financially supporting the communities they are trying to sell their products to, especially those who put rainbows or other signals on to increase sales!

What guidance would you give to other current/future business leaders about why being LGBT+ inclusive matters?

I think being accepting and affirming is non-negotiable. What we do as communicators is so important and we have to have a variety of perspectives included in the crafting of messages for any brand or business or service or individual. You have to start from a place of having all of the voices heard. This is a strength and I believe now a requirement to be effective communicators and branders and strategists moving forward. Being mindful of one's own bias and of a company's bias – and recognizing when there is only one type of person in the room – means you create even better work product and better results for your clients. You have to make sure that the people in the room are diverse in their backgrounds because it brings a fuller understanding of the needs of clients and the audience. It used to be optional, but now we see that there is no longer a tolerance for tone-deafness. There is no longer an option to be one-note.

Bill Barretta

Writer, Director, Producer, Consultant and Core Performer with The Muppets
white, cisgender man (he/him), heterosexual

Bill Barretta is a world-renowned Muppet legend. He has portrayed Earl Sinclair on Dinosaurs, Clueless Morgan in Muppet Treasure Island, and he has developed and created many beloved characters. These include Pepe the King Prawn, Johnny Fiama, Howard Tubman, and Bobo the Bear. He has also taken over several of Jim Henson's characters, including Dr. Teeth, Rowlf the Dog, Mahna Mahna, and Swedish Chef. His producing credits include It's a Very Merry Muppet Christmas Movie and The Muppets' Wizard of Oz. In addition, he has consistently served as Muppet Captain, leading all Muppet performers during a variety of projects including The Muppets and Muppets Most Wanted.

Please share your story

I don't know if I would consider myself a "leader"? I suppose it depends on what you believe a leader is. There are of course, good, and bad leaders. I believe over time I have established myself as a person who offers a "Respected, Collaborative Guidance with the utmost Integrity". That's my reputation. My industry is all about reputation, as I believe should be the case for any industry, organization, or community. I believe without respect, collaboration, and integrity there can be no real guidance or "leadership". Sorry, to be political for a moment, but look at our country today.

I try to carry on by example, using the various traits from others who have also led me, by example. My parents, grandparents, my brother, Uncles & Aunts, teachers, acting mentors, peers, industry idols and many friends have all been inspirational in their own unique way.

I've always pretty much been a sponge, and so the challenge for me has always been to figure out which are the best traits to completely absorb from others and which to just wipe up and ring out along the way. I've also tried to take advantage of opportunities that opened up along my journey so far, that would eventually or hopefully allow me to be in a position of "guidance".

Though I didn't know at the time where these various opportunities would lead me, I genuinely and generally followed my heart. I followed something I learned early on, which is to follow the path that you truly love, and the rest will follow. Otherwise, what's the point? The most important sub-traits of this type of guidance that I describe, I believe, are honesty and working harder than anyone else. You can't expect more from others if you don't expect the same, and even more, from yourself.

I believe it's those two traits that makes others feel safe with me when being offered or placed into a position of guidance. Whether it has to do with dealing with a budget, troubleshooting issues, creative solutions, or motivating others—without those two sub-traits, I can't deliver to the best of my ability and that's what everyone needs and is looking for in the end.

What do you remember about your early experiences or considerations for LGBT+ people in your industry?

I happen to believe that my industry was built and founded in the hearts and on the shoulders of people who had the amazing passion for the arts and lifestyle of the LGBT+ community, before it was called the LGBT+ community. Unfortunately, LGBT+ people in entertainment history, my family and friends have very slowly been accepted over time and are still challenged by many who are ignorant and closed off to the larger, more inclusive vision.

I recall when I created a character back in 1996 for a show called "Muppets Tonight" named Howard Tubman. Because this character came from me and not someone else like a writer, I felt that Howard was a gay man, or actually, a gay Muppet Pig ... literally a pig animal.

I debated with writers and producers to not outright say or try to infer that Howard was gay in dialogue or during scenes that he may have been in, but rather, to let the character speak for itself and leave it open to the public's interpretation. There hadn't been a Muppet that was considered gay and I know that it made some people very nervous at the time. Even some of my gay friends. But I had to stay true to the character.

This character was based on a real person I knew growing up in the 70's. My mother was a model, and he was one of her friends in the fashion industry. So, I knew this person, and he was a good hearted, entertaining personality that I'll always remember as an artistic and fun influence. My intention was never to insult or demean him in any way. In my heart, Howard is the same kind of tribute as my character, Johnny Fiama, is to my father. I love Howard and I believe now, over time, people have learned to love him for who he is and not judge him by his perceived sexual orientation, or by their own stereotypical views and personal perspectives in life.

What have you seen change since then?

I believe I've seen a continued growth in understanding and celebration in my industry. There will always be those who lack basic empathy shrouded in ignorance for others, whether it's about the LGBT+ community or another group of individuals. But I'm proud to be a part of an industry that celebrates all types of people because that's just what we do. We occasionally get to shed light on topics that people are afraid to talk about or confront. People live vicariously through my industry because it allows them to experience for a moment what life might be like as another individual you never thought you could understand or relate to. Sometimes it opens their eyes when they least expect it. I love that we can have that kind of effect on others.

That's the beauty of acting and creating characters like the Muppets. We can be anything from a charismatically egotistical, Spanish King Prawn, named Pepe, to a proud and fantastically talented, gay Pig, named Howard.

Everyone is welcome and accepted with the Muppets and I'm extremely fortunate to live amongst them.

Where do you think your industry or company will go next in terms of LGBT+ inclusion?

Hopefully, my industry will continue to move in the same direction that it seems to have taken for many years now and continue on into the future. I believe it will. Broadening even further their accepting minds.

What guidance would you give to other current/future business leaders about why being LGBT+ inclusive matters?

Well, why I believe it matters, is very simple, but yet extremely complex still for so many. It's simply about seeing people as people, first. Everyone should be equally valued the same as a human being, first. Maybe individual's skills are different, or their artistic ability varies, but we must never judge people on their origin, race, religion, sex, or beliefs. Otherwise, you could be missing out on the greatest, most influential, moments of your life.

People tend to try and formulate ahead of time, what they believe matters or how they're going to judge or be judged by others. They try and prepare or plan what they think is best, or what's going to happen "if I do this or say that". Well, one of my favorite sayings that I live by and that has served me well in my decision-making is, (and I'm not even a religious person), but it's this … "Wanna make God laugh? Tell him you have a plan."

Think about it … we're all inclusive and we really don't have a choice. Only you can choose to be heartless, ignorant, and blind.

Greg DeShields

Executive Director at PHLDiversity, a business development division of the
Philadelphia Convention and Visitors Bureau
African American, cisgender man (he/him), gay

As Executive Director of the Philadelphia Convention and Visitors Bureau PHLDiversity, Greg is responsible for developing and implementing plans, strategies and initiatives specifically designed to raise Philadelphia's image as a diverse multicultural destination leading to hotel room nights and economic impact for the region. Greg is a Graduate of Johnson & Wales University Providence, Rhode Island, with an A.S. Degree in Hotel & Restaurant Management; and B.S. Degree in Hospitality Management. Professional Development Leadership Graduate: Institute for Diversity Certification, Urban League of Philadelphia, Leadership Forum, Leadership Philadelphia, and Greater Philadelphia Leadership Exchange.

Please share your story

I have always had a desire to build my career in the Hospitality and Tourism industry. Originally, I thought the path to career success would be in an operational capacity managing a hotel. While in college I was educated/advised to pursue my career as a manager/leader beginning as a management trainee. After graduation, I entered a hotel company management training program which was a priceless career opportunity.

After working in various management capacities in hotels, I had what I called my "mid-life crisis" at age 37, realizing I wanted to do more, shaping the hospitality industry rather that working in a single hotel property. I then transitioned into a non-profit organization leading a department, I narrowed my focused as a leader driving the direction of an organization. This led to finding the key to my career success passion, which I also feel is the core of a great leader, endless motivation to achieve a professional and organizational goals in collaboration with incredible teams and partners.

What do you remember about your early experiences or considerations for LGBT+ people in your industry?

Figuring out how to not promote my sexual orientation to fit in. It was a common occurrence to strategically use vague pronouns and not discuss my personal life.

What have you seen change since then?

You can completely be your entire self, I never felt as whole as I do now, I can contribute the best of personal and work life, think more inclusively, experience personal and professional pride.

Where do you think your industry or company will go next in terms of LGBT+ inclusion?

The industry will continue to be more inclusive, as more LGBT+ leaders are in key roles and become owners of hospitality establishments. Additionally, as more legal determinations are passed in favor of the LGBT+ community, we will experience greater equality.

What guidance would you give to other current/future business leaders about why being LGBT+ inclusive matters?

Being LGBT+ and supporting us matters because our voice is stronger together, also the more we are represented the more we influence decision, present real role models, and make a difference.

Richard Gray

Senior Vice President, Diversity, Equity & Inclusion for Greater Fort Lauderdale Convention & Visitors Bureau
white, cisgender man (he/him), gay

> Richard Gray is known as the "Godfather of Gay Travel." Under Richard's guidance, Greater Fort Lauderdale was the first tourism board to start an LGBT+ department and remains the only CVB in North America with a department designated solely to LGBT+ outreach. Four years ago, under his leadership and guidance, Greater Fort Lauderdale became the first destination in the world to create a transgender marketing campaign. Now the Greater Fort Lauderdale Convention & Visitors Bureau includes trans, lesbian, gay, and straight people in all its mainstream marketing initiatives.
>
> He is an inductee in the IGLTA (International LGBTQ+ Travel Association) Hall of Fame, a Fort Lauderdale Hometown Hero, and a recipient of the Gay+ Award for Achievement from MTV/Logo. In 2016, Q. Digital gave Richard an honorary award for his commitment to transgender tourism. In 2017, the United Nations highlighted his transgender destination leadership. In 2018, he received the Stonewall Visionary Award and in 2019, Richard was recognized with the HERO Award from the Greater Fort Lauderdale LGBTQ+ Chamber of Commerce. He's been named one of the most influential business leaders in South Florida.

Please share your story:

My personal journey in this ever-evolving platform happened fairly organically. In 1991, I moved to Fort Lauderdale from New York City where I had a successful career in Investment banking on Wall Street in the 80's. I struggled with being in the closet in this male macho dominated world and yearned to be "me". I fell in love with Fort Lauderdale, the beach, the waterways, the weather, palm trees and I felt drawn to move there. There was something that told me Fort Lauderdale was going to become a world class destination. I decided to retire from banking, change careers and enter the world of hospitality. At that time there were only a couple of gay accommodations, all rather grungy and not appealing to me. It was then than that I decided to create and open The Royal Palms in Fort Lauderdale. The first luxe upscale gay accommodation in the world. An oasis where gay men could be themselves and escape from being pseudo straight in the mainstream working world. Within a short period of time, I had elevated the standards of gay accommodations globally and without realizing it and was putting Fort Lauderdale on the map as a destination for gay travelers to visit. To this day it is the most Awarded and written about gay hotel and featured in the news media globally.

In 1993 I was elected to the Executive Board of Directors of the International Gay Travel Association, which later on became the International Gay & Lesbian Travel Association. I became one of the longest running Board members ever. It was an exciting time. This was when corporate America started to look at the gay market and DINKs. (dual income, no kids) IGLTA went from a tiny Association with several hundred members of travel agents, tour operators and gay guesthouses to around 1,000 members. I became a key face and voice in the global lesbian and gay travel world. Corporate America saw the importance of that economic spend. Gays traveled, not only for business but for pleasure and when they traveled, they spent money eating out, going to bars and shopping. Corporate America realized we were an important market segment to reach.

I became the spokesperson for the destination Fort Lauderdale because I had this international platform. This fueled my passion, and I went on as many global panels as I could. I looked for any chance to speak about Fort Lauderdale because I had a vision for this destination, and I was keen to share it. In the 90s, this city wasn't among the hot gay destinations like Palm Springs, Miami, and Provincetown. I wanted a voice at the table and wanted to educate not only the travel industry, but everybody, that Fort Lauderdale was an option. It was a destination that was growing and emerging and had hundreds of gay-owned and operated businesses.

I formulated relationships with people around the world from my early days as spokesperson for the destination. In 1995, I sat down with Nicki Grossman, who at the time was the president and CEO of the Greater Fort Lauderdale Convention & Visitors Bureau. I wanted a familiarization gay trip for IGLTA to come to Fort Lauderdale and showcase the destination. Seventy travel agents and operators came, and that's when my involvement with the Greater Fort Lauderdale Convention & Visitors Bureau really meshed. These agents and operators saw how amazing the "Venice of America" was and how incredible our beach was. They had only associated us with spring break previously and didn't realize our nightlife was so good. This catapulted us towards becoming a top LGBT+ destination in the USA and later on, the world.

I became the CVB's liaison and created a rainbow campaign for the CVB which launched in 1996. I became a spokesperson again in an organic way. I also became the first openly gay person to Chair the Marketing Advisory Committee and then became the first gay to be Vice Chairman of the Tourist Development Council. My role as the liaison grew and grew. I sold The Royal Palms in 2008 and then began working for the CVB. My mandate was to continue to develop and grow lesbian and gay tourism as well as create an awareness of how diverse and inclusive this destination had become.

We were the first CVB with a dedicated LGBT+ department with the focus to grow LGBT+ tourism and awareness of our destination among the LGBT+ community. I define myself as an early pioneer in LGBT+ travel and am happy to use my platform to educate others.

What do you remember about your early experiences or considerations for LGBT+ people in your industry?

Coming from England I was raised by parents who did not see color or religion. Reality hit me hard when I moved to New York City and I realized how America was so bigoted. It was a great shock and took me a very long time to tolerate. In 1982 the AIDS epidemic was exploding, and gay men of all ages were dying. They were also being ostracized from society. I became an early volunteer for Gay Men's Health Crisis under Larry Kramer in New York City and Captain of Buddy Team 6. I wanted to help people with Aids and I also wanted to be a voice educating people that you could not contract AIDS from just touching a gay man or drinking from the same glass. It was a deeply emotional time of my life, especially when my best friend Aldo died in my arms from AIDS. I lived in New York City in the 1980's and tragically I lost all of my friends to AIDS. I will never forget the 80's!

All my life I've always had this desire for equality, inclusion, and acceptance, and I've pushed for this from as early as I can remember, because it was how I was raised. I grew up in Europe, and I wasn't used to the hatred that I saw happening in the U.S. In 1992 after opening The Royal Palms I had a gay tourism interview with *Miami Herald*, but I told them not to mention my name. Looking back, it was a missed opportunity. There is the power of the press. I realized I needed to share my voice and use all platforms given to me. I realized the power of those interviews would educate mainstream people and LGBT+ people. I have had some hate mail and even eggs thrown at my gate at The Royal Palms. Overall, most feedback I've received was always positive. I knew early on the press was important, and I continue to share important messages and stories through the press. The press became my voice and strategically I was grateful that they listened to me. One of my strengths is I'm good at building longstanding relationships, and I'm loyal. I don't think of the destination first, I look at the bigger picture. It's about all of us sharing knowledge and being successful.

What have you seen change since then?

Thanks to my broad vision and influence Greater Fort Lauderdale is committed to breaking down gender barriers and leading the global travel industry towards greater inclusion of ALL people, regardless of religion, color, sexual orientation, or gender identity. We are global leaders in this platform that many destinations look towards for leadership and direction.

Four years ago, Greater Fort Lauderdale became the first destination in the world to create a transgender marketing campaign that was actually recognized by the United Nations. Now the Greater Fort Lauderdale Convention & Visitors Bureau includes trans, lesbian, gay, and straight people, as well as people with disabilities and of different sizes in all its mainstream marketing initiatives. We are continuously working to reach the LGBT+ community to show them we are a destination that is diverse, welcoming, authentic, and accepting. We have been honored to welcome the Southern Comfort Conference, the largest annual trans conference in North America, to our destination for several years now.

Greater Fort Lauderdale is the LGBT+ capital of Florida and one of the top 7 LGBT+ destinations in the US, per Community Marketing, Inc. We pride ourselves on our diversity and inclusion and being such a welcoming destination to all travelers. We especially pride ourselves on being the global destination leader in Trans travel. Our latest campaign and best to date is called "Celebrate YOU" and in this campaign, we include Trans, Drag, Lesbian, Disabled, Non-binary and gay in a very non-resort way. We're leading and making a difference among the industry and our campaigns are thought provoking.

There are 4 fundamental human rights:

1   The right to equality and freedom from discrimination.
2   The right to freedom of expression.
3   The right to life and liberty.
4   The right to privacy.

It is essential to suffocate all the hate and the discrimination that is out there with leadership, awareness, light, tolerance and most of all, visibility. Under the TRUMP administration, the United States was temporarily no longer the beacon of freedom and justice that it used to be, and I feel ignited and empowered to fight even harder for global change and acceptance within and around the LGBT+ community. The word diversity demonstrates that every person is unique and brings something special and different to the table. Inclusion is the step that leads the way to awareness, and in turn leads to greater acceptance, and then leads the way to ending discrimination. None of us are free until we are ALL free.

Where do you think your industry or company will go next in terms of LGBT+ inclusion?

From a marketing and PR perspective the global trend is unquestionably all about Integration. We have to thank Associations like the National LGBT Chamber of Commerce in Washington, D.C. for educating corporate America of the importance of Diversity, Equity, and Inclusion. I believe that solely LGBT+ is a thing of the past. Re-invention for destinations and corporations/businesses is essential for them to survive and thrive. Corporate America is our greatest ally, and we all have to thank them for their leadership in diversity, equity, and inclusion.

As greater acceptance of diversity and inclusion becomes more of the norm, I believe that destinations will integrate their niche markets, just as we did 5 years ago, the first destination in the US into their overall mainstream campaigns. I think that in 10 years' time there will be less of a need for specific LGBT+ campaigns. I see LGBT+ travel becoming more integrated into mainstream. People want to be around all people. We are a destination that has broken down barriers. Our destination has been talking about LGBT+ travel since 1996, and we were way ahead of the curve.

Diversity is a meandering journey and love knows no boundaries and it is absolutely critical for all of us to use our own personal platforms to maintain the rhythm and drumbeat for advocacy, global rights, equality, and inclusion. Inclusion is making the mix work and it is a continual work in progress. Promoting and protecting the human rights of all people regardless of their sexual orientation or gender identity is absolutely critical. Silence can equal death and it is absolutely unacceptable to be killed because you are LGBT+. There are more than 70 countries where being LGBT+ is banned. The hospitality industry is the first to feel the impacts of unrest and uncertainty in the world. The traveling public looks for value and safety when making their travel decisions. Our industry is facing this challenge more than ever in the United States under our current administration in Washington. In Greater Fort Lauderdale, we are making sure we let the traveling public across the world understand that WE have an open-heart and open-door policy to ALL people across the world, regardless of the color of their skin, what religion they believe in, who they choose to love or how they choose to identify.

Is genderless the global future we ask ourselves? A gender-less future is not one where we don't have gender, it's one where gender doesn't impact access or respect. Greater Fort Lauderdale believes that it most definitely has merit. We should "de-gender" travel to better educate people and celebrate Transgender and non-binary people and show that we are part of an accepting, inclusive, and transformative world? After all gender is an integral part of this destinations core identity.

What guidance would you give to other current/future business leaders about why being LGBT+ inclusive matters?

The LGBT+ market is a vibrant market that should be embraced, understood, respected, and marketed to in an appropriate manner with careful attention being paid to gender nuances.

Diversity is not just a word or a sign on the door, it is not only a way of living, it is a way of doing business - the right way! It is imperative that we educate, elevate, energize, and inspire ALL people, especially LGBT+ allies. Visibility creates awareness. Awareness leads to acceptance. And widespread acceptance ends discrimination. You can't change hearts, minds, and attitudes if you are invisible. Visibility advances acceptance, and I never intend to be invisible. Rest assured Greater Fort Lauderdale will always push the envelope. I look at it like this. Diversity is being invited to the dance. Inclusion is being asked to dance. Greater Fort Lauderdale is a destination where everyone is free to dance. Be proud of who you are and who you love ... love knows no boundaries and should never be a privilege.

Sally Hogshead

Founder and CEO of How to Fascinate
white, cisgender women (she/her), heterosexual

> Sally Hogshead is a best-selling author and one of the world's most sought-after speakers. Sally has won more awards than any other advertising writer in the U.S. and was called "the most successful junior copywriter of all time." Hogshead's books include the top-selling *Radical Careering: 100 Truths to Jumpstart Your Job, Your Career, and Your Life* and *Fascinate: Your 7 Triggers to Persuasion and Captivation.* Her book *How the World Sees You: Discover Your Highest Value Through the Science of Fascination* was on the New York Times Bestseller List. Her next book, *Fascinate, Revised and Updated* was on the New York Times Bestseller List, and a #1 Wall Street Journal Best Seller. Sally's groundbreaking research into the science of fascination includes national studies with over a million participants. Sally can describe exactly how your own individual personality is most likely to persuade and captivate any prospect within 9 seconds. Based on her company's (How To Fascinate) proprietary research, Sally created the world's first assessment based on branding (rather than psychology).

Please share your story

All of my work is based on my belief that to become more successful, you don't have to CHANGE who you are. You have to become MORE of who you are.

After graduating from Duke University with a minor in Gender Studies, I skyrocketed to the top of the advertising profession, becoming the most award-winning copywriter in the United States by age 24 for brands like Nike and Coca-Cola.

Since then, I have measured the personal brands of over a million professionals, and published two *New York Times* bestsellers in 22 languages. I am a member of the Speaking Hall of Fame, the speaking industry's most illustrious award for professional excellence, been featured by the *Wall Street Journal* and *Oprah Magazine*, and have twice been named the world's #1 Global Brand Guru.

What do you remember about your early experiences or considerations for LGBT+ people in your industry?

In 1995, I started my career as an advertising copywriter. The experience was like the TV show "Mad Men" (but a few decades later!). I loved agency life and tapping into the cutting-edge of trends and culture. Agencies separated consumers into very specific demographics. Diaper ads targeted new mothers, whereas cruise lines targeted retirees.

Looking back, I realize now that the LGBT+ consumers were very rarely taken into consideration. Sure, you'd see a pride flag tossed into the ad's design here and there, but generally LGBT+ consumers were marginalized as a fringe culture. It was seen as an obscure category. An outlier segment. A box to check on a media plan.

Today that seems crazy. For a few reasons.

First, from a business perspective, there's the sheer financial spending power: In 2019, LGBT+ consumers spent $3.7 trillion globally. Ignoring how roughly 5% of the U.S. population identifies is insane.

But more to the point, gender identity and sexual orientation is not some obscure category on a spreadsheet. For most, it's a key driver of decisions and passions and sense of self. Being gay is not a superficial mindset or fashion statement. Being transgender is not a trend or passing fancy.

This ignorance on the part of the marketing industry is very, very telling. Here's why.

Advertising leads the cultural conversation, staying on the edge with progressive ideas and messages. The whole purpose is to embrace trends and the motivations behind them. So, it wasn't just ad agencies marginalizing the LGBT community, but commentary on the social conversation in general at that time.

Happily, things have changed. Marketing messages today are far more inclusive and empowering of diversity. (And thanks to advocates like Kryss Shane, we keep improving!)

What have you seen change since then?

I shifted my focus from studying *brands* to studying *people* and their personal brands. Since then, I've measured the personal brands of over a million professionals globally.

In my research inside companies like Twitter and NASA, I discovered a secret …

High performers do not excel by competing on the basis of being BETTER. Instead, they tap into what makes them DIFFERENT.

It's good to be better. But it's better to be different.

Different is better than better.

So, what makes you different? This is a question for us all to consider, and not just the LGBT+ community. We all can tap into our unique, innate specialties. Just as brands must differentiate themselves, so must we all. I developed a personality test that measures what makes you different, and how to apply your most valuable traits. Too often, among teams, diversity is spelled with capital "D," with air quotes. However, true diversity isn't a committee, a training manual, or a department. It's a new norm.

Where do you think your industry or company will go next in terms of LGBT+ inclusion?

When my child came out to me, my inner mamma bear reared up a stunning ferocity.

Today, I feel a similar protectiveness for the gorgeous (yet marginalized) variety among us all. We need to not only protect and nurture diversity, but to also send a clear message:

You don't have to CHANGE who you are. You have to become MORE of who you are, at your best.

Justin Nelson, the Co-Founder & President of the National Gay and Lesbian Chamber of Commerce, says this beautifully:

"You don't have to hide a part of who you are to be successful in your business. Leaders don't always realize the power they can harness by authentically embracing inclusion."

Failing to understand each person's greatest unique qualities means you will fail with profits, customers, teams, and engagement.

To help answer this question, my team and I have started developing training programs about bringing forth every aspect of diversity.

My new focus is helping teams and organizations rise to their highest potential with a system to shift the mindset away from traditional performance, and toward showcasing their most authentic and differentiated personal brand.

What guidance would you give to other current/future business leaders about why being LGBT+ inclusive matters?

If you only remember one thing, remember this:

Different is better than better.

Kenny Johnson

Community Engagement Coordinator Philadelphia Phillies
Black/Asian, cisgender man (he/him), heterosexual

> *As the Community Engagement Coordinator with the Philadelphia Phillies, Kenny Johnson plans and promotes outreach and community events at Citizens Bank Park and throughout the City of Philadelphia to keep the Phillies connected with Philadelphia's diverse communities. His work is founded on the belief in creating opportunities to deliver world-class fan experiences while celebrating Philadelphia's diverse communities and continuing that constant vibe of inclusivity.*

Please share your story

I started with the Phillies while still in high school, serving as an intern in Outreach and a game day worker. I continued the internship each summer while in college and was hired full time a few years after graduating. From there I had been involved in the planning and implementation of a variety of programs geared towards youth and evolving baseball fans. I now plan and promote outreach and community focused events, as well as help keep the Phillies connected with Philadelphia's many great diverse communities.

What do you remember about your early experiences or considerations for LGBT+ people in your industry?

Since the time that I first started working for the Phillies, I was fortunate to find that the environment and culture within the organization was very open and inclusive, with a handful of LGBT+ employees in a range of positions in the company hierarchy. That environment has maintained and flourished since then, with an additional few LGBT+ employees joining through the years.

What have you seen change since then?

In addition to the above, through the years I have also seen this inclusive culture spread outwards towards our fanbase and our community, with a growing number of relationships with LGBT+ community organizations and institutions, higher involvement in LGBT+ community events, a structured celebration of Pride month and Pride campaigns and events at the Ballpark during the year, and collaborations with Major League Baseball initiatives towards inclusiveness and towards spotlighting the contributions of the LGBT+ community.

Where do you think your industry or company will go next in terms of LGBT+ inclusion?

Within the baseball industry, the trend slopes towards even greater LGBT+ inclusiveness, as Major League Baseball has an established and dedicated Office of Diversity and Inclusion, responsible for leading the industry towards greater diversity and representation within its workforces, business partners, initiatives, and events.

What guidance would you give to other current/future business leaders about why being LGBT+ inclusive matters?

LGBT+ inclusivity is not only a moral imperative, but a business imperative as well. It has been well documented that businesses with greater diversity are more likely to perform better than their counterparts with less diversity. And with the trend of many industries moving towards greater inclusivity, there will continue to be a higher focus within these industries on better connecting with LGBT+ communities when attracting workforce talent and potential business partners.

Shelly McNamara

Human Resources and Equality Executive Proctor & Gamble
white, cisgender women (she/her), lesbian

> Shelly McNamara is the Chief Equality & Inclusion Officer at Proctor & Gamble. She also serves as a member of the World Economic Forum's Community of Chief Diversity & Inclusion Officers, the Conference Board's Global D&I Executives Council, and the Cincinnati Chamber's Minority Business Accelerator. In addition, she is a sought-after speaker on topics of diversity, equity, and inclusion on mainstages throughout the country.

Please share your story

I am an open and proud human being. I identify as lesbian, and my wife & I have three grown daughters (all three are now in their 20's). I grew up on the west side of Cleveland, Ohio in a large Irish Catholic family. I grew up at a time when being LGBT+ was judged harshly everywhere around me—media, friends, family, and religion. I began to come out when I was in my late 20's after years of internalizing the shame that others had thrown my way. It was at that point that I decided the only way I could live my life was authentically as the person I was created to be. When I made this choice, I finally felt free.

It wasn't until my mid 30's that I came out fully at work. I came out because my wife & I made one important decision—"our children would not learn shame from us", so once we were expecting our first child, I fully shared who I was with work colleagues. Our journey as a lesbian couple and parents of three daughters has had its challenges—but it has been marked mostly by the many friends and family members that have stepped up to love us. Those who chose to not support us have missed out dearly.

I work in the profession of Human Resources and Equality. The empathy and insight I have gained from my unique family, and the experience of being marginalized, has made me a better HR professional. My journey has also deepened my desire and commitment to learn more about racism and sexism. I am committed to create an environment of respect and equality for all. There are deep and challenging issues of inequality in our country that need our attention.

What do you remember about your early experiences or considerations for LGBT+ people in your industry?

My company has been on an accelerated journey to expand equality and respect for members of the LGBT+ community. I have been privileged to be part of the core group that has made important interventions:

- We built an Ally strategy that invited in our straight colleagues to learn more about us and be a voice for us. We asked that they take actions to eliminate barriers in our way.
- We convinced the company to change policies that enable members of our community to have access to the same health care coverage, parental leave, and relocation benefits.
- We have done training & capability building that opened hearts and minds—and educated our fellow employees about who we are in this broad and diverse community and sensitized them to the unique barriers that members of our communities face.

What have you seen change since then?

I interact regularly with senior people from companies across the US and outside of the US (Spain, Costa Rica, Germany, Brazil, England) who are doing work in their companies to bring about more equality and respect for members of our LGBT+ community. We continue to find the "next wave of change" that is needed to keep making progress.

Where do you think your industry or company will go next in terms of LGBT+ inclusion?

The next generation of work is to get more visible LGBT+ people at the most senior levels of corporations. This is where strategy and resource ownership lie. It's important that the youth see models for who and how they can become.

What guidance would you give to other current/future business leaders about why being LGBT+ inclusive matters?

It's essential that each human being lives their truth—being and living true to who you are. It's only by being true to yourself and living the life you were meant to live that you will find joy and offer your gifts to the world around you.

We in the LGBT+ community have gifts to offer the world. If we can all commit to create our workplaces, neighborhoods, and communities as places that ensure respect and support for all—the world will be a better place.

Brian McNaught

Corporate Diversity and Inclusion Trainer
white, cisgender man (he/him) gay

Husband to Ray Struble; Managing Director of Global Equity Sales for Lehman Brothers
white, cisgender man (he/him) gay

Brian McNaught has been named "the godfather of gay diversity training" by The New York Times, Brian McNaught is considered one of the world's leading corporate diversity consultants dealing with lesbian, gay, bisexual, transgender, and queer issues in the workplace. His book Gay Issues in the Workplace is in the Library of Congress. The Human Rights Campaign provided a copy of the book to members of Congress. His web resource has been licensed by Microsoft, Citi, Chubb, Merck, and others. He has written a total of eleven books and has seven DVDs, many of which are used as college texts. Much of his material has aired repeatedly on community access television stations throughout the nation, training and educating countless people.

Please share your story

I was fired for being gay by the Catholic Church in Detroit in 1974. I was 26. I was a weekly columnist and reporter for *The Michigan Catholic*. My column was dropped because I was featured in a *Detroit News* story on homosexuality and religion. I had started the Detroit chapter of Dignity, a gay Catholic organization. I went on a subsequent hunger strike that lasted 24 days, ending when the bishops pledged to educate the clergy. I was later fired.

My husband Ray was, when he retired at 45 in 1977, a managing director of global equity sales for Lehman Brothers. He was, to my knowledge, the first openly gay person on the trading floor in any company, and, in 1991 was the openly gay head of Lehman's Atlanta office.

In 1986, I became the first person to do LGBT+ diversity training in a corporation (Bellcore). I subsequently was called "The Godfather of gay diversity training," by *The New York Times."* I received a standing ovation from the National Security Agency's senior leadership. I have written numerous books and website resources, along with videos and DVDs, all to provide LGBT+ trainings to companies worldwide.

Prior to my retirement from road travel, Wall Street companies had brought me to speak in their offices in Mumbai, Tokyo, Singapore, Hong Kong, Melbourne, Sydney, London, New York, and throughout Canada. In the Asian places, it was the first time an openly gay person had spoken on gay issues in the workplace.

What do you remember about your early experiences or considerations for LGBT+ people in your industry?

Bellcore, Bell Labs, and AT&T, my first three clients, all required their employees to take eight hours of diversity training a year. My workshops were eight hours long and were conducted for all shifts in the manufacturing plants. The business imperative that I created for the first training in 1986 was, "In the war for talent, in order to attract and retain the best and brightest employees, and to optimize productivity, companies have to create a workplace in which every employee feels safe and valued."

From the very beginning, I had to address the issue of conservative religious beliefs. I would announce from the start of each session, "This is not about changing your personal beliefs, but rather about treating everyone with professional respect." To the issue of whether an employee could be forced to attend the training, I suggested the manager say, "I can't make you go. I'll be disappointed if you don't go, and you will be held accountable for everything that is taught in the training. If you act in a way that is thought to be disrespectful, or unwelcoming, you can't plead ignorance."

What have you seen change since then?

I always recommended starting the training with the Executive Committee. The only way to bridge the gap between corporate policy and corporate culture is through education. Putting a face on the issue is the most effective way of helping employees understand the impact of an unwelcoming work environment on LGBT+ colleagues. If training begins at the top, it will be taken more seriously by middle managers.

An example of the environment on the factory floor was offered in a workshop with third shift employees. One man said, "If someone came out to me, I couldn't guarantee they wouldn't lose their hands in a machine." Posters announcing the workshop in various corporations were defaced. A sign was hung on the door of one of my workshops. It was from the Bible, Leviticus 18:22, "A man who lies with a man, as with a woman, is an abomination." In one site, early on, I had to take off the seats anti-gay literature that had been left prior to the workshop.

One of my powerful tools in helping employees understand the fear of coming out began with me asking them to raise their hands in response to a couple of questions. The first was, "How would you describe the environment where you work for lesbian, gay, bisexual, and transgender employees? Is it—Very Welcoming, Somewhat Welcoming, Somewhat Unwelcoming, or Very Unwelcoming?" White collar workers usually voted toward the "Very Welcoming" end of the spectrum. I'd then ask, "If I came out to you, what do you think would be the best thing for me to do, stay in the closet at work, come out to a few close friends, come out to my manager, or come out to everyone?" I'd explain the "coming out to everyone" wasn't using a bullhorn in the hallway. It was leaving a picture of your partner on your desk. Again, managers almost always said, "Come out to everyone."

A little while later in the same training, while discussing "heterosexism," I explained that it was a value system that believed it was superior to be heterosexual, but it was also an assumption of heterosexuality unless we're told otherwise. I'd ask the group how many people thought they could pick out a gay person. The group agreed that it's hard to do, and that some heterosexual people had stereotypical gay affectations. I then said, "I'm very good at picking out gay people, and I'm going to do that now." Suddenly, the room got very quiet.

I would acknowledge the silence and ask why there would be fear that I'd name you as gay if it wouldn't be hard to be gay at work, as they earlier claimed. We then processed all of the assumptions people would make about the people I said were gay, and how their workplace would feel different. That moment of fear that they had that I was going to pick them out as gay helped them understand why gay people are afraid of coming out. People would often come up afterwards and comment how that experience of anxiety that I would name them as gay helped them understand the need to proactively create a welcoming environment.

I then told them of how the day after I spoke at the NSA, I got an e-mail from a senior person that said he had followed my suggestion of talking about my presentation at home with his family, and that an hour later, his daughter walked into the bedroom and said, "Dad, we need to talk. I'm a lesbian." The NSA manager responded, "Thank you for telling me," as I had instructed, and said, "you changed our lives for the better. My daughter and I embraced and cried."

Where do you think your industry or company will go next in terms of LGBT+ inclusion?

Mostly, what gay and transgender people feared, and continue to fear, despite all of the advances, is, "If I come out, will I be treated differently?"

In helping employees see the value of my corporate presentation, besides making the business case, I'd explain that the information would make them more culturally competent with their children and grandchildren. I used the elements of songs to help them examine what vibes they give off on the issue. In a song you have words and music. The corporation has words on the subject, promising in print that they don't discriminate on the basis of sexual orientation or gender identity. But what music do people feel in their workplace? I suggested that I could read their comfort level with the subject by observing their body language. That is part of our music. The words may say we're safe, but we feel otherwise. The same is true at home. Your words to your children are, 'I love you. I want you to be happy," but what's your music?

What guidance would you give to other current/future business leaders about why being LGBT+ inclusive matters?

Gender identity and expression was a brand-new subject when I made it part of my training in 1986. As a trained sexuality educator, I was able to help employees understand the differences between sexual orientation and gender identity, as well as the differences between biological sex, gender identity, gender role, and gender expression. Today, we need to add to our discussion the concept of binary, and non-binary thinking, and the significance of pronouns.

It's my experience that ignorance, or lack of familiarity, is the parent of fear. We often fear what we don't understand. And fear is the parent of hatred. We often hate what we fear.

People are neither good nor bad. We make good choices and bad choices. The choices we make are influenced by our awareness.

Jerrie Merritt

SVP Community Development Manager, Bank of Nevada
Black, cisgender women (she/her), heterosexual

> Jerrie Merritt is the Senior Vice President and Community Development Manager for Bank of Nevada. Her work includes the progression and coordination of all community development activities, as well as working collaboratively with state and local agencies, nonprofit development groups, and other participants in community and economic development programs and projects. Her primary focus is to strengthen existing client relationships and building strong community partnerships. She was awarded the Women of Distinction Award by the National Association of Women Business Owners (NAWBO) and was featured as an Interesting Personality in the Inaugural Edition of Who's Who in Black Las Vegas™ and chosen as a Woman to Watch in 2016 by Vegas Inc.

Please share your story

Over the years, I've had the opportunity to speak to many groups, mostly women, about finances. Women are in charge of more money than men are! Quite often, I start to talk about myself and I always begin by sharing that I am the illegitimate grandchild of a sharecropper. My grandfather could not read or write but was the smartest man I've ever met. I was raised by my grandparents because my mother had me at age 13. My grandparents believed strongly in education. They knew it was the key to open the door to get out of Alabama and out of the environment I grew up in, one in which I remember drinking fountains for colored people only and where movie theaters were separated by race. All of my life, we never owned land. Getting my education was very important. Still, by the time I graduated from high school, my concept of going to college was almost impossible because my family could not afford college. My then-boyfriend (now husband of 47+ years) entered the Air Force, which led us to wed and this offered me the opportunity to leave Alabama. Before leaving, I had to promise my mother that I would become as educated as my new husband and I could afford. This began with signing up to attend school where we were stationed, though the coursework was inconsistent as I had to work to save up for each class before I could enroll. In the third year of marriage, I had my child and we moved to Fairbanks, Alaska. I had a few credits in a business degree and still needed to work to save up for each class I wanted to take. A friend suggested I apply for a job at the local bank, though I had no experience. I hesitated but applied. Surprisingly, I was hired. I became a bank teller and continued to go to school, this time at The University of Alaska. The bank paid for classes as long as they were finance-based, so I majored in Business and Finance.

By year #4, I became a branch manager because of my education and my drive to want to be a leader. Every time there was an open position, I would always apply. This led me to run my own branch. I was putting down roots. The Air Force had other plans. Off my family went to Las Vegas, Nevada. I immediately applied for a manager position but was denied. I was only hired as a teller. Six months later, when I applied for the management-training program and was denied, I left and went to another bank. It was the best decision of my life, though I could not have known it at the time. (In hindsight, I was the only Black woman who applied so this was likely due to discrimination, though this was not something I recognized at the time.)

It has been almost 40 years since then. I have held a number of leadership roles, including Executive Vice-President titles. I now work as the Senior Vice President of Community Development Manager. In short, I am a person who gives the bank's money back to the community. I get to use my experience in my own life and in my own community to better the world around me. I get up every day loving the work I do, something I never thought I would get to do.

When I think about LGBT+ inclusion, I think about my own life experience. My younger brother was gay. As a family, we spent too much time not admitting this was his truth. By the time we were honest with ourselves, we had very little time with him. He died of HIV+ related complications after becoming infected through his partner, someone else we did not get the chance to know well because of our long-time denial. As my brother became sicker and sicker, many judged him. Many judged us for loving him. When I think back, just the thought that he could not tell his family, that the person he loved died, that he went through all of this almost completely by himself changed me. Thinking about how much time we could have spent loving him instead of trying to so hard to deny who he had changed me. It changed me in ways I cannot articulate, but the idea that a loved one did not feel fully loved through the entirety of his life made me forever different. My level of acceptance for LGBT+ people is deep within me, not because people had to teach me with words, but because love had already taught me.

When I encounter someone who is LGBT+ identified, I do not only accept the parts of them that are just like me. I do not pretend not to know parts of who they are. I recognize that they are whole people and that they are people worthy of kindness, respect, compassion, and love. I no longer deny their identity, and this allows me to have deeper stronger relationships both personally and professionally. Yes, it makes the world safer for them, but it also makes the world better for me. Accepting and Affirming others is not just a kindness we give to others; it is a gift we give to ourselves. I am certainly a better person for this and that absolutely translates into the workplace, where I am a better leader to those who never have to worry about being authentically themselves at work.

What do you remember about your early experiences or considerations for LGBT+ people in your industry?

It had never been something people have openly discussed; it was just known that this was not something people shared about themselves. I have known many who have worked in the banking industry for decades, some of whom I know are LGBT+. However, it has always been an unspoken knowledge that no one asked, and everyone knew better than to ever share.

What have you seen change since then?

I have seen tremendous changes in the industry, starting with the larger institutions, Wells Fargo, Bank of America, Citi Bank, Chase … their diversity and inclusion programs started because of their LGBT+ employees. Now it's more about racial diversity, but the foundation for the LGBT+ community is largely the reason why the larger banks have such strong diversity and inclusion programs. If you were to ask me, as a leader, why, I think it's obvious to leadership and to management that the sexual orientation of an employee does not tell you the value of their work. At the same time, if those employees are happy with who they are, the work a leader can get out of them, the work the employee gives to the company is so much greater than if they have to be concerned about their bosses finding out who they are.

Do I feel that the inclusion of LGBT+ people in the financial services industry has reached a level where it is not as big of an issue as it once was? Yes. They are so far ahead of other areas of other areas of diversity and coming together to support other areas (such as racial diversity) matters now more than ever. However, we still see primarily white men and white women in leadership. We don't know everyone's orientation or gender identity, but it is obvious that change needs to come.

Where do you think your industry or company will go next in terms of LGBT+ inclusion?

I would say that LGBT+ people have made bigger strides in some areas of the financial services industry than racial groups, largely because it is easier to hide sexuality or gender identity than race. I see continued acceptance coming and I hope that leadership becomes better at embracing ALL areas of diversity in its representation. However, this is dependent on the geographic location and the specific company. This needs to become more universal on every level of leadership throughout every financial corporation including banks, gaming, and other aspects of the industry. Opportunities to grow, be mentored, and become high level leaders still need to become more common. While it is now less likely in many areas for immediate job loss, I think we are still working to improve how we gain public support for diverse groups. I think this will continue to grow as leaders promote and encourage acceptance and support for diverse groups. I sit on committees and push for this myself. I think other leaders will continue to see that we have people in our organizations and corporations who bring value, not because or in spite of their LGBT+ or racial identity.

What guidance would you give to other current/future business leaders about why being LGBT+ inclusive matters?

I would tell them that it matters because every individual that works for your company, whether in financial services or another industry, they matter. If they matter to you and if you value that person because they have the ability to help you grow your company, to make your company better, being able to let them be who they are brings the value to you that you couldn't get any place else. Is it important? It is very important. I think it is more important today for corporations to embrace diversity and inclusion than it has ever been before because, in the past, I think employees were not willing to let their employer know who they truly were. Because of diversity and inclusion, employees who work for any organization want to be included. In order for them to be included, the organization needs to embrace who the individual employees are who work with us and for us. I truly believe that LGBT+ people -and members of other marginalized communities- needs to feel included because that is who they are. We do not have the ability to change them and, if you expect them to perform at the level you pay them at, it is so important that you include all of who they are as individuals.

Gary Murakami

Director of Global Sales, MGM Resorts International
Asian, cisgender man (he/him), gay

Gary Murakami is regarded as one of the Hospitality, Hotel and Convention Management industry experts in hospitality sales and convention services. He is the Director of Global Sales at MGM Resorts International, which operates a portfolio of destination resort brands including Bellagio, MGM Grand, Mandalay Bay, Aria at City Center and The Mirage. With more than two decades of hospitality experience, he provides an expertise in a variety of sales and sales leadership roles, including corporate transient, leisure, and group with past management experience of a large team of tenured sales professionals. His hotel experience is a unique blend of industry experience at Fortune 500 International Hotel Chains of Marriott/Ritz-Carlton, Hyatt Hotels & Resorts, Four Seasons Hotels & Resorts, and the current role with MGM Resorts International. He currently collaboratively manages and represents over 3+ Million in Convention and Meeting Management Space for the MGM Resorts International's portfolio of distinguished hotels.

Please share your story

An engaged and passionate industry professional for more than twenty years, I have been an active participant within the industry with experience in many roles in sales and sales leadership. My hotel experience is a unique blend of industry experience at some of the leading hotel chains including Marriott/Ritz-Carlton, Hyatt Hotels & Resorts, Four Seasons Hotels & Resorts, and the current role with MGM Resorts International. This holistic vision of the many facets of the industry has provided key insights and viewpoints, which I have had the pleasure to share with our industry community through my longstanding commitment and spirit of volunteerism. I have also pursued many industry specific certifications and education to elevate my experience and share its importance to the visibility of the industry and increase its view and professionalism.

I have always had a passion and interest for the hospitality industry. Growing up, my mom had worked in various food and beverage positions in restaurants and hotels, and I specifically remember vividly the experience she had working for hotels. As I pursued other opportunities in different industries following college, I returned back to my passion for travel and hospitality. I realized a career that connected with my personal passions would create a professional future that was sustainable and provided the most longevity and growth.

Being an engaged and active participant within my industry has been a personal and professional mantra throughout my entire career. I have always encouraged others to stay engaged and be a part of the change and excitement within the area of meetings and events industry within the greater industry.

Life presents many challenges and obstacles along the way that sometimes impacts our journey and the spirit and commitment to volunteerism has been a constant for me. I feel that throughout my career, I remain amongst a few individuals that has been steadfast and unwavering in my lifelong commitment and involvement with the industry. In reviewing and reflecting on my 20+ years in the industry, I am particularly proud that I have never not volunteered in any single year. I remained focused and committed that being involved and engaged were critical to my professional career growth, and I often share these sentiments of being involved with others in the industry.

What do you remember about your early experiences or considerations for LGBT+ people in your industry?

My earliest experiences and considerations were that our LGBT+ community had always been an integral thread of the hospitality industry. I believe that a sense of community along with the opportunity to seek and to find other LGBT+ people provided an even greater incentive to pursue my career in hotels. Unlike other industries where barriers needed to be broken or limits pushed, I initially selected this industry as I naively felt it was "safe" and provided an opportunity where I feel I could bring my authentic self to work each day without discrimination or harassment.

As an early Generation Xer who witnessed our LGBT+ community impacted by the AIDS crisis, I found an initial sense of solace to be fully engaged in a career and industry where I could find other like-minded individuals. Although I found it to be almost "stereotypical" in many ways to pursue a career within hospitality and travel, I was not "brave" enough in my early years of my professional development to want to break ceilings and impact change.

Much of this self-doubt in my early career also stemmed from a lack of confidence which only in part was a result of self-identifying as a gay man of color. The "struggle" was not important enough then to have motivation to try anything different as I feared professional setbacks or lack of advancement. Even today, self-doubt happens, and I seek to "catch myself" into falling into any chasm where the voices in the back of my head influences set-back.

What I did find, however, from my experiences over the years is that barriers and ceilings do exist also in these traditional industries that are viewed as more "LGBT+ friendly". Being gay and a person of color often entered into my frame of thinking and in many ways on occasion still casts a shadow creating a sense of unknown as to whether lack of advancements earlier was a direct result.

As I matured into my career, I strategically sought out companies that aligned with my personal and professional values and reflected a culture where one can bring his/her own authentic self to work each day. I find that while businesses do have expressed policies of an open culture, many companies self-admit that there still remains work to be done. Generational and culture shifts in recent years has influenced the importance of LGBT+ individuals to pursue careers and companies that align with one's one values and embraces the complete individual.

What have you seen change since then?

The hospitality industry has been some of the strongest advocates for supporting and embracing the LGBT+ community in recent years. Earlier in my career more than 20+ years ago, the travel industry was in its infancy in its approach to LGBT+ business and the understanding of the market. Once further research and articulation of the intrinsic economic significance of the LGBT+ market became recognized, more hospitality companies began to deploy further efforts and initiatives to address and to support the LGBT+ community.

Societal values also have changed in the past decades. With the recognition of gay marriage and other rights of the LGBT+ community became more mainstream, the hospitality industry along with many other industries recognized its support of the LGBT+ community including its own employees became critical and essential to business and commercial success.

Where do you think your industry or company will go next in terms of LGBT+ inclusion?

Creating a culture of inclusiveness and diversity and promoting its value is paramount and essential to the continued growth and development of our industry. It is only through supporting different voices and experiences can we stimulate continued creativity and sustainability for the industry.

It is by "lifting up" and by engaging with different thoughts, experiences though a culture and industry of inclusivity, that we can amplify these voices and provide more conscientious role models and opportunities.

As the hospitality and travel industry is focused on "hospitality", it is imperative and necessary that our industry will continue to lead the way to break down barriers and across communities. The hospitality industry will serve as a conduit to bringing people together and embrace the diversity of individuals and create environments of inclusiveness.

I feel that my overall achievements and engagement through industry involvement and leadership has impacted the overall hospitality industry, and specifically the area of meetings and events, as I have been able to leverage my experience and involvement across various aspects of the industry to contribute a holistic and collaborative strategy. I feel that I have served as a role model for the future of our industry and represent the diversity of our community as an LGBT+ person of color. My involvement and visibility as an engaged member of our meetings & events industry will hopefully inspire others that their individual voices are important and critical to the fabric of our industry growth and sustainability.

What guidance would you give to other current/future business leaders about why being LGBT+ inclusive matters?

Being an actively engaged, passionate and authentic individual in the industry is a frame of reference and thought that can be universally applied to other individuals and organizations inside and outside of our industry. When there is focus on inclusion as a behavior, diversity will inherently result from this mindset. I am convinced that the hospitality industry's approach to develop an "inclusive, equitable and diverse" culture can lead to transformational growth and development toward social and economic change.

The conversation that must happen is for us to find our voice, and it is the responsibility of each of us to be an active participant within our respective industries as well as outside of our professional careers. Our hospitality industry has a tapestry of faces, experiences and history that are not always recognized or realized. All of these voices are critical to the sustainability and growth of the industry, and we must amplify these ideas and thoughts to move our community forward.

Alfredo Pedroza

Senior Vice President of Government Relations, Wells Fargo
Latino, cisgender man (he/him), gay

Alfredo Pedroza is a seasoned twenty-five-year veteran in community, government and public relations and public policy. Working at the intersection of non-profit, government and the private sector, Alfredo brings a passion for social justice and equity and believes that business can and should be a catalyst for social good. Understanding that community, constituents, and customers drive market and political forces, Alfredo has honed his ability to anticipate trends, manage risk and build solid and authentic relationships. Alfredo has worked as the Mayor's Liaison for District 9, 11, and the Latino Community Office of Neighborhood Services in San Francisco. He currently sits on the boards of the Mexican Museum, Honor PAC, and Equality California, and he bikes to Los Angeles from San Francisco every other year to raise money and awareness to end AIDS.

Please share your story

Growing up in San Francisco during the height of the gay liberation movement, when people were coming to San Francisco from all over the world to come out, I was the gay Latino kid from the Mission, growing up in a conservative family going to Catholic school. (not every neighborhood in SF at the time was a Pride Parade). I had to leave San Francisco to come out and to discover who I was. I did that and then came back to finish college and begin my career. For me, it became a process of slowly coming out in concentric circles, family and then friends, and eventually co-workers. Initially, I was out to everybody, but I was not out at work. I realized there were things I could not contribute or participate in because I was not living authentically. When I made the conscious decision to be out at work, everything changed; relationships deepened, negative assumptions I had about others and they had of me disappeared. It allowed me to be true to myself, fostered deeper relationships, made me a better collaborator, and it gave me the opportunity to think about things differently. It let me grow my professional network through authentic connections and conversations, which led to opportunities in the future.

My career took off when I became honest and forthcoming about who I was and the importance of my perspective through my lived experience—the more I shared the more my perspective was sought after in my professional circles. It worked to motivate me to find places to shine, seeking out organizations where I could bring my full self to work. From my work in non-profits, to the work I did in government working for the Mayor of San Francisco, to working for a Fortune 20 Financial Services company I realized that representation matters. Living authentically and living proud has presented opportunities that otherwise would not have happened including the biggest highlights of my career if I had not been open to sharing who I was. I believe every opportunity has built upon each other.

Working for San Francisco headquartered bank, being out and gay wasn't groundbreaking. Wells Fargo had a long history of support for its LGBT+ employees, customers, and communities. Bringing my entire self to work wasn't a question it was an asset. While not perfect, Wells Fargo was in many ways more ahead of the curve than most of our peer banks. Even still, I was the first out gay person and one of two people of color in my group 10 years ago and now one of three LGBT+ people and one of three POC in the group, when we would meet at industry conferences the lack of LGBT+ and BIPOC representation would be mainly from our bank. While my experience as an out gay Latino has been mostly positive it hasn't been an even experience for everyone, black and brown and trans people in corporate America have had to face tremendous systemic barriers to advancement.

What do you remember about your early experiences or considerations for LGBT+ people in your industry?

What I remember most was that an LGBT+ person was invited and then you were expected to do all of the work to educate everyone else on our diversity dimensions and do double the work to feel "included". We felt like quotas. It was our job to stay included, to get to be in the room. Having perspectives, sharing opinions, being truly included in the finished product was a lot of effort all the time. Opportunities to be mentored or sponsored were not as readily available and allyship was not yet as defined.

What have you seen change since then?

I think it varies from industry to industry, company to company. In some environments, it has become more authentic and more efforts are made to create environments that are safe and welcoming. However, the work can't ever stop. Some companies still struggle to even start the work, others think a one and done approach is sufficient. I think we are making progress on the L and the G but lots of work still needs to happen on the B, the T, and the + parts of our community, especially when it comes to the additional diversity dimensions of BIPOC. Many people saw it as a check the box (some still do), but it shouldn't just be the responsibility of diverse people to educate the rest, everyone needed to have a role in inclusion so that is systemic and authentic.

Where do you think your industry or company will go next in terms of LGBT+ inclusion?

I think my industry still has a lot of work and a lot of reckoning to do. There needs to be more mentorship. There needs to be more sponsorship at every level of the company. As any industry, we have to do better to reflect the communities we serve. It has to be the goal to reach that place, where there is more equity in representation in every aspect of a company's operations and at every level all the way up to the C-Suite.

It reminds me of Justice Ginsburg who once said that, to paraphrase, if there are nine seats on the Supreme Court, she'd see nothing wrong with nine of them being filled by women, as no one batted an eye when they were all men. Diversity and inclusion is only a zero-sum game if we allow it to be, I think we have been conditioned for far too long to think of it that way and I think its way past time to challenge that and reimagine how we think about it.

What guidance would you give to other current/future business leaders about why being LGBT+ inclusive matters?

In so many places still an LGBT+ and or BIPOC person is still the first or the only in their department or their company or to receive an award to reach a certain level. What I say to those people is that we must work to ensure that we are not the last, we need to be stewards of the opportunities that we had access to and pay it forward. Its everyone's job to be inclusive and representation matters it is vital to a future economy and to our society's future! Diversity of thought and perspective leads to more creativity and better business outcomes and a much less boring world.

We spend a lot of time in this country assimilating so that we can fit a mold. I so much wish someone would have told me growing up that being unique and living your authentic self would be so valuable in the work you create and the gifts you bring to all you do. Your perspective is value. Bringing your entire self to your work is better for everyone! Being thoughtful and authentic is critical!

In terms of the individual who is not LGBT+- inclusion is not an option anymore. It is a benefit to get perspective in all areas of business, from marketing to creating content to product development to messaging, you have to include the LGBT+ perspective. LGBT+ people are trendsetters, they set the stage for what will be hot next. If you're not in that space, you're already behind! Companies that do not seek out diversity, won't ever have the environment in which it will thrive and won't attract it. No one should have to work hard to fit in at work! If a person has to work hard for that, they cannot do the hard work required of them to do their real job, which harms the entire organization. Inclusion is an opportunity to let people blossom in the workplace and to contribute to the business objectives. If you want richer conversations and bigger and bolder ideas that resonate with the marketplace, inclusion is absolutely necessary!

Howard Ross

Best-Selling Author, Sought After Speaker on Leadership, and co-founder of Cook Ross and Udarta Consulting
Jewish/white, cisgender man (he/him), heterosexual

> Howard Ross is a lifelong social justice advocate and is considered one of the world's seminal thought leaders on identifying and addressing unconscious bias. Howard has been the recipient of many awards, including the 2009 Operation Understanding Award for Community Service; the 2012 Winds of Change Award from the Forum on Workplace Diversity and Inclusion; the 2013 Diversity Peer Award from Diversity Women Magazine; the 2014 Catalyst Award from Uptown Professional Magazine; the 2014 Catalyst for Change Award from Wake Forest University; the 2015 Trendsetter in HR by SHRM Magazine; and the 2016 Leadership in Diversity Award by the World Human Resources Development Conference in Mumbai, India. He was also named an Honorary Medicine Man by the Eastern Cherokee Reservation in N.C. and given Medicine Holder designation by the Pawnee Nation.

Please share your story

It was very organic! My parents were pretty liberal for their time and from a family that suffered enormous loss during the Holocaust. When I was growing up, I got involved in the Civil Rights movement at a young age, then went fully into1960s activism: Civil Rights, Anti-Vietnam War Movement, the Farmworkers Boycott and got to meet some major activists when I was pretty young. After college, I wanted to do meaningful work, so I started to work in a childcare center and spent 13 years as a teacher and then administrator. When I took over running the school, I tripled it in size in one year through implementing what I learned while studying organizational leadership and culture change. This resulted in significant school success, which led to my being asked for my guidance and advice via workshops put on for others wanting to make their businesses more successful.

Word spread and I began to be asked to guide corporate partners. I then left the school to do this full-time. Through this work, I was asked to run a hospital program, which had been designed by Robert Allen, who taught me about organizational culture change. By then, it was the mid-1980s. Through my work and continued activism, I was connected with others who were leading the charge on diversity in the workplace. There were a lot of assumptions about race being the reason for some's success, rather than their capacity, which minimized their abilities and undermined their importance. It was really hard to watch, and it further fueled my passion for my work, as I realized that this incorrect belief pattern harmed everyone.

I started Cook Ross in 1989 and the business grew. During that time, I found myself troubled because I was struggling to reach those who needed to learn about diversity and inclusion, but they were not so interested. When I became accidentally exposed to unconscious bias research in the mid-1990s, things began to make more sense as to why people were hesitant to want to grow and change, as well as how to guide them effectively. This heavily informed my personal understanding and significantly shifted the focus of my work.

I specialize in the synthesis of neuro-cognitive and social science research and direct application re: Diversity, Inclusion, Equity and Accessibility work. My client work focuses on the areas of corporate culture change, leadership development, and managing diversity. I have successfully implemented large-scale organizational culture change efforts in the area of managing diversity and cultural integration in academic institutions, professional services corporations, Fortune 500 companies, and retail, health care, media, and governmental institutions in 47 of the United States and over 40 countries worldwide. In addition, I have delivered programs at Harvard University Medical School, Stanford University Medical School, Johns Hopkins University, the Wharton School of Business, Duke University and Washington University Medical School and over 20 other colleges and Universities. I have also served as the 2007–2008 Johnnetta B. Cole Professor of Diversity Professor of Diversity at Bennett College for Women, the first time a white man had ever served in such a position at an HBCU.

My work has been published by the Harvard Business Review, the Washington Post, the New York Times, Fast Company Magazine, Diversity Women Magazine, Forbes Magazine, Fortune Magazine, and dozens of other publications. I have appeared monthly on National Public Radio and served on numerous not-for-profits boards, including the Diversity Advisory Board of the Human Rights Campaign, the board of directors of the Dignity and Respect Campaign, and the board of the directors for the National Women's Mentoring Network.

I am also a former Rock 'n Roll Musician and have taught meditation and mindfulness for more than 20 years, including my role as co-founder and Lead Facilitator for the Inner Journey Seminars. I founded Cook Ross Inc., one of the nation's leading Diversity and Inclusion consultancies. He sold the company in July 2018 and founded Udarta Consulting, LLC.

I now keynote and speak regularly at Conferences for SHRM, SHRM Diversity, the Forum for Workplace Inclusion, National Association of Corporate Directors, ATD, the World Diversity Forum, and dozens of others.

In the talks I give and the books I write, I mentor others through focusing the work on realizing that this is usually not a problem of whether someone is a good person or not, but rather on their need for help seeing the world with self-awareness and a willingness to confront and adjust their biases. As a result, people became more interested and engaged in my work, which led to more talks and trainings, which led to my first book "Reinventing Diversity" (2011) and its success led to "Everyday Bias" (2014). Over time, my company continued to grow. I sold the company in 2018 and released "Our Search for Belonging" about tribalism that same year. All three have been widely successful, which shows that people really do want to learn and improve. Since 2018 I've continued to work toward social justice through my writing, speaking events, and mentorship.

What do you remember about your early experiences or considerations for LGBT+ people in your industry?

When I was younger, there was very little open expression of sexual orientation, certainly here in Washington DC and Maryland where I was growing up. However, as many inherently do, I had some internalized homophobia. My big awareness started to happen in the early 1980s as I met more openly gay people through my teaching work and later through my other life experiences. I began to wonder about the experiences of LGBT people, and this led me to ask a gay male friend to spend a day with me in the city as if we were partners. We did not do anything extreme, we simply walked around for a day sometimes holding hands or standing quite close to one another, wearing pro-Gay t-shirts. While I don't pretend that this equates to people's day to day experiences, it allowed me to experience a day in his life and the prejudices and microaggressions that gay men experienced. I was blown away.

The level of distain and judgment was profound ... as was realizing that I'd had no idea. For him, it was an ordinary day. For me, it was anything but. This helped me to become more of an LGBT+ activist. I always believe that, once you start paying attention to a social injustice, you can't not. I began to see it everywhere and that led me to speak out to people and to include it in my work. About 1/3 of the time, someone after one of my talks would approach me and come out. Some even did during my talk, coming out to their workplace for the first time. It was both moving and a sign that I was having the impact that I was aiming for. I maintained this belief and intention of inclusion within my own company, Cook Ross, which became known as a place that was safe for LGBT+ people to work. When I sold the company in 2018, About 20–25% of the company's employees were LGBT+ identified. For me, this is just part of life and it wasn't about them, it was about me recognizing my unconscious bias and changing my perspective and becoming more aware.

What have you seen change since then?

One of the things I've learned about life and human transformation is that it is not linear. We start on the outer circle and return to the outer circle, but each revisit is hopefully more evolved in how we learn and how we deal with what we struggle with. In the early days, the focus was on race and racial injustice only, then we evolved and became more focused on race as well as on men and women interacting with one another. Then LGBT+ people began to live more openly, and it turned into a deeper conversation about sexual and gender identity. At the same time, the work began to become shortened when businesses wanted talks that were shorter and more focused on business impact than on personal change. Now, we have been circling back to the profounder work and the deeper personal growth and understanding. The arc has come back to deeper explanations. This can be scary for people, leading to backlash, which is dangerous, but it is also just a part of the growing and evolving process.

Where do you think your industry or company will go next in terms of LGBT+ inclusion?

As Dr. King said, "the arc of history bends towards freedom." Women's rights and racial justice and LGBT+ inclusion in America are better than they've ever been … though there's no question they are still nowhere near where they need to go. We just have to keep finding ways to accelerate the change. How do we continue to do this? We keep at it. We recognize what comes up next as a form of bigotry and we fight this as it begins, and we work to prevent it from taking root as we also work to end what biases have been strongly rooted. We have these patterns that happen and sometimes politicians contribute to trying to resist or stop this change, but we see that it's only a matter of time before the change becomes more rooted than the bias.

Most likely, the industry will continue to grow and evolve as we move to encourage the voices of marginalized groups to rise. As this happens, it helps us all to better understand where we can learn and what we did not know about the life experiences of those unlike ourselves. Sometimes, sadly, change and conversation happen after tragedy. As I've said in my books, inevitably, people will have bias and our tendency to divide between us and them, which is inherent to human behavior. It is up to us to deal with this constructively.

What guidance would you give to other current/future business leaders about why being LGBT+ inclusive matters?

I think one of the real important things to consider is intersectionality. We have long dealt with groups as monoliths, but this is inaccurate and unrealistic to keep doing. We will continue to see more people in marginalized groups in the media and in leadership roles. It will become impossible to ignore. The more we see each other for *who* we are, the less we treat each other like *what* we are. For future leaders, I encourage and recommend that you wake up and realize that your inherent or intentional bias is discarding a group of humanity. Whatever the percentage of a marginalized group within larger society, even the smallest percent of people is a lot of people. When you are intentionally not looking at that and when you are not consistently working to reexamine and unlearn your biases, you are allowing people to suffer, and you are feeding the tendency for people to have to be hidden to be safe. This undermines their performance and their willingness to stick around in your company, neither of which result in a business' success or in your success as a leader. In my own experience of running a company, with so many people being "out" without fear of impunity, we got higher levels of performance and the business significantly benefited. To not realize this is just foolish. The bottom line is this: Diversity, Inclusion and Belonging are just good business.

Josh Scott

Lead Pastor, GracePointe Church
white, cisgender man (he/him), heterosexual

> Pastor Josh Scott has been a pastor for twenty years. He currently serves as the Lead
> Pastor at GracePointe Church, a leading progressive Christian church in Nashville,
> Tennessee. GracePointe Church has been at the forefront of the movement of inclusion
> and affirmation in Christian contexts. Before coming to Nashville, he spent fourteen years
> leading a progressive church in rural Kentucky. Josh is an active voice in the conversation
> of imagining the future of progressive Christianity and seeks to make those concepts and
> ideas practically accessible. He and his wife are also foster parents.

Please share your story

My grandfather was a Freewill Baptist Pastor. Those experiences were not
a fit for me. But I gave my first sermon when I was 17 on a Sunday night,
during a youth service. I was asked to give a sermon because the Pastor saw
me as a leader (though I did not at that time), but I said yes because I
always say yes to people. I was so concerned about it, but the reaction was
strong both from the audience and from me. Over time, I began to travel to
places where Pastors were out sick or traveling and I've been traveling and
giving sermons ever since. I think good sermons are part stand-up comedy
and part theology. My first official role was at age 20.

In the late 90s I decided that I would dedicate my life to working in
churches. I pastored a couple of small churches in college. In 2005, I moved to
lead a non-denominational church in rural Kentucky. I was there for 14 years.
The first thing we dealt with was that our church was not inclusive; we had a
church statement that did not allow women to be in leadership roles.
Together, we changed that. After, we became openly LGBT+ affirming. It
caused some people to leave us, but it also caused some people to come!

The rise of Trump in American politics led me to become more openly
political and more vocal. I would not tell my kids that I stood silent, saying
nothing, out of fear of losing my paycheck. I decided to keep speaking up
for them and for all of us.

What do you remember about your early experiences or considerations for LGBT+ people in your industry?

I was raised to read the Bible a certain way, literally, and the thing
everybody said about loving the sinner and hating the sin was always there.
I can't pinpoint a moment when I decided to walk away from that old

non-affirming view and become affirming. I had friends I knew who were coming out whom I knew as good people and I could not justify the theology saying there was no place for them when there were some mean selfish people who were allowed to be in the church. It made no sense that just because someone happens to be LGBT+ means they do not get to be a part of the church. It sent me back to the Bible and to read books about the Bible.

My grandpa would not accept my theology, but I've learned that I can honor the experiences of my spiritual ancestors without embracing their explanations. Theirs put us on the wrong side of biology, science, theology, equality, and more. They had valid experiences, absolutely, but we have to adjust what we do based on what we learn and know. It does not undermine or undervalue their contributions; we just know more now than we did, and we have to adjust as we learn.

What have you seen change since then?

Many are learning what I have; that we don't need the Bible to tell me that same-sex relationships were holy because people I saw in the church were committed, faithful, and loving. I don't need the Bible to tell me that's okay, it's beautiful. But I do think we've misinterpreted the texts that are often cited from the Bible, known as the "Clobber Passages." The Bible does not talk about a faithful committed relationship between people like we are talking about today. We have evolved in our relationships since then. Abuse and human trafficking and other older ideas and ideals in the Bible are obviously not a fit for today, why do we assume other things aren't in need of reconsideration too? Why should I stand in front of the church and tell people they must reject their child? Why would I harm by encouraging people not to accept their loved ones? Why would the Bible ever be used to harm people?

I think there is a growing awareness of this and that the number of people will keep growing and keep affirming. I also know that it's a challenge for some church leaders because they feel they have to be quietly accepting because they fear that being openly inclusive may alienate some of their conservative donors. However, I think more are following our faith in prioritizing people even though it may feel like a risk.

Where do you think your industry or company will go next in terms of LGBT+ inclusion?

I think it's hard to tell at this point. We still have churches in small groups or areas with very narrow understandings of humanity, where women cannot be leaders, where the views are still racist, sexist, and generally antiquated. I DO think the majority of the churches will come around to inclusion. We have already seen Pope Francis come around and speak up. I wish he would have said not only that it's okay but that churches would serve them communion and bless their marriages. Affirm that they can teach and lead in the Church. Also, back up and ordain women priests. Also, let's end priesthood celibacy. We have to go back and fix so many problems here as well as moving forward and addressing more recently recognized inclusion!

As we move forward, Pope Francis will likely lead the Catholic church into a more inclusive space. I see inclusion happening more and more. I know the majority of people support LGBT+ people. It means that church has to either change or become irrelevant. It isn't us changing to fit the culture, it's that the culture saw things and were more accepting before we were. Culture educated us and heard Jesus and God better than the Church. We need to listen.

What guidance would you give to other current/future business leaders about why being LGBT+ inclusive matters?

I would say that you can't "have do" it. You can't say "we just don't want to see it" or "as long as they don't talk about it" about this. What happens when the "don't ask, don't tell" type of church policies exist? You can't be half including people. You have to make a stand and go all the way, include the community in every possible way, without barriers to involvement or engagement. They can serve where they're gifted, in any staff or volunteer position. It has to be full inclusion.

If you commit your life to love and inclusion and believe that all people deserve love, you'll be in situations where courage is a necessity. Know what hills you are willing to die on. This, for me, was one of them. Knowing that there is a cost when you buck the dominant traditional religious paradigm has to be considered. However, there is such a reward; human beings being loved and knowing they are welcome is a gift to be able to watch and to facilitate that. Seeing someone who had been harmed by the church become trusting again because your church is safe (because you make it so) is such an incredible gift.

Andrea Shorter

Inclusion Strategist and LGBT+ Pioneer
African American, cisgender women (she/her), lesbian

Andrea Shorter has more than 35 years of experience as an advocate and strategist for social justice and the empowerment of women, LGBT+, and people of color. A widely regarded and respected voice on the socio-politics of race, gender, sexuality, equity, inclusion and diversity, Andrea has appeared in numerous media, and as a featured speaker and panelist on these matters. Andrea's work as a longtime leader, advocate and strategist in the lesbian, gay, bisexual, and transgender liberation movement is extensive, including NAMES Project Foundation/AIDS Memorial Quilt, Equality California Institute, and Out & Equal Workplace Advocates. Andrea is a longtime Commissioner on the Status of Women for the City and County San Francisco. Her public service career started soon after her graduation from Whittier College as an aide to a California State Assembly Legislator. She was awarded a David Bohnett LGBT Leaders Fellowship at the Harvard Kennedy School of Government.

Please share your story

While I've lived in California for the better part of my life, I hail from Indianapolis, Indiana. I was born into a loving, caring family that held conservative religious values, and as a young black girl, I was more or less expected to behave, live by, and value prescribed and somewhat rigid gender roles. Be gracious, be feminine, speak my mind, but ultimately submit to the will and authority of men. However, I was an independent minded, curious, strong willed, and mentally gifted child. As such, one is constitutionally predisposed to question nearly everything about them. And, I do mean, everything. Further, I suppose, mostly for my personal safety, when out in the world, at play, at school, at market, I was also expected to live by both the formal and informal rules prescribed for living while black in a predominately white, in many regards, segregated society. Which basically amounted to always be pleasant, congenial, non-threatening. Suffice to say, I didn't manage well by either prescription.

As a young Black girl growing up in the 1970s, I was also interested in what I read and saw in the current events concerning the women's liberation movement. I enjoyed the intellectual propositions about equality of the sexes. While I was young black person, few people in my family or community were directly involved in the recent events of the 1950s-1970s Civil Rights movement, so there was little firsthand experience shared or imparted to me about fighting for, standing up for equality of any kind. So, my best exposure to any robust discourse about equality was about equality of the sexes via the women's rights movement.

My first attempt to activate for equity and inclusion was in the 7th grade. Back then, when there were required home economics classes, only girls could take home economics, and only boys could take wood shop. I neither understood nor believe that this imposed class segregation by sex was right, necessary, nor, practical. In protest, I refused to complete my cooking and sewing assignments, organized a few other girls to stand with me, and made demands known to the teacher and to the principal: Girls should be allowed to take shop, as boys should be allowed to take home economics. While I made my protest known, and won a few allies, and perhaps even the hearts and minds of some teachers and administrators, 7th grade home economics was the first and only class I would ever fail in my entire academic life! Still, it was worth it in ways I could not have imagined. The feeling of pride, possibilities, promise in my stand for my own and that of others potential, and self-worth has lasted and inspired me throughout my lifetime.

From that experience, I think I enjoyed most that other kids—not many, but a mighty few—stood with me. We were a movement. Eventually, a few years after our action, girls could take wood shop, and boys could take home economics—or both. By then, however, I had graduated middle school, and my father moved our family to California.

My journey as an LGBT+ civil rights advocate began as a college student in the 1980s, during the era of the HIV-AIDS crisis. Because I came out during this period, I consider myself a "Silence = Death" kid. Silence equals Death was a rallying cry to heighten the visibility of then-often closeted LGBT+ people. Being 'out' came with great risk. Even in the 1980s, just as it had been for decades before, out LGBT+ people or people thought to be LGBT+ could lose everything: you could lose your job, you could lose your family, you could lose your children, you could lose your life to violence. In some states, you could be imprisoned or institutionalized for being homosexual. Once you are out, there's no turning back. So, coming out, being out was a big deal.

To an extent, the presumed and real lack of visibility of LGBT+ people allowed for negligence and lack of much needed government response to what was clearly an epidemic that was taking the lives of gay men, and people of color. I came out because I wanted to be out, not live in the shadows, wanted to be free to be who I am. It was important in that moment in history to be known, visible, and standing with and among other LGBT+ identified people and allies in the movement to demand a response to an epidemic killing people.

To this day, these were some of the bravest, most courageous Americans I believe I shall every meet. We were literally fighting to save our lives.

Since then, activating for HIV-AIDS response and other justice causes not only makes a difference for my own sense of well-being but as importantly, if not more, knowing that it can make a bigger difference to fight for those who cannot speak up, who cannot directly lend their voices for needed change.

What do you remember about your early experiences or considerations for LGBT+ people in your industry?

I've covered a lot of ground in 30 plus years as a strategist and advocate for criminal and juvenile justice reform, gender equity, LGBT+ rights, including same sex civil marriage equality, civil and human rights. It's been an honor to advocate from various platforms including program development and management, non-profit executive positions, and even elected and appointed official posts. If I've learned anything from a hybrid experience, there are always opportunities to build new partnerships to advance good work.

At the end of the day, no matter our differences—by race, religion, political affiliations, gender identity, sexual orientation—there is more we have in common than that we do not. Most of us want to see each other be safe and prosper, find happiness, live in good health, thrive as a valued contributor to community. Recognizing these commonalities is a start to positively advancing an inclusive workplace or environment for everyone.

What have you seen change since then?

While the hard-fought battle for same sex civil marriage equality is now won, and the right to civil marriage is now the law of the land in all 50 states, a misperception is that the fight for LGBT+ rights is over, that we are covered, and have been accorded all civil rights and protections. This is not the case, and far from being the case.

LGBT+ people's lives, safety, and security are still very much at risk. Even with some level of federal protection against discrimination, laws vary from state to state regarding the extent of prosecution for discrimination against LGBT+ people or even people thought to be LGBT+. For instance, in some states, as recently as mid-2020, you could get married on Sunday and then go into work on Monday and be fired for being out as LGBT+ or suspected of being LGBT+. Even with federal protections, the continued existence of racism, long after federal racial policies have been enacted, indicates that we are far from safe and far from supported while in the workplace.

So, while LGBT+ visibility might be greater than ever in popular culture, as central characters in television shows, in cinema, as talk show hosts, as pop music stars, news anchors, etc., and more people are out as supportive family, friends, and allies of LGBT+ people, we are still not protected or seen as equal under law. The passage of an Equality Act would help to ensure those protections are in place, similar to the Civil Rights Act of 1964.

Businesses that are workplace inclusive in all fifty states are important partners that challenge such discrimination. When a CEO of a major company like Salesforce, Apple, or Angie's List challenges LGBT+ discrimination in a locale where a branch or outfit of their company exist, local and state leaders listen. When CEOs lead by example by ensuring their company and supply chain is LGBT+ inclusive, that impact is far reaching. It impacts the lives and career opportunities of LGBT+ employees, it can increase productivity, it can impact and even change state, local and even regional policies and practices concerning LGBT+ inclusion.

Where do you think your industry or company will go next in terms of LGBT+ inclusion?

Advocates will continue to work with companies and business leaders to support their efforts to create LGBT+ inclusive workplaces. We will continue to develop the technical assistance, organizational capacities, data and research, and other resources that can support business to be successfully inclusive.

What guidance would you give to other current/future business leaders about why being LGBT+ inclusive matters?

Discrimination is bad for business. It is costly and benefits no one.

Business leadership that invests in racial, gender, gender identity, sexual orientation discriminatory practices, is failed business leadership.

Business leadership that understands, embraces, and values inclusion and diversity of experiences and backgrounds as added value, a strength, and foundation upon which to build and sustain enterprise is rewarded by stakeholders, shareholders, supply chains, consumers, clients, customers, and by and large the communities in which their businesses are located.

Discrimination and failure to be inclusive, diverse just furthers wastes of time and resources that could have been better spent on investing in the potential of human capital it takes to innovate, compete, and succeed. I often think of what life can be like in the year 2050, in a vision of having relieved ourselves of the fears, prejudices, discrimination, and barriers that have prevented our collective and individual evolution for far too long. What would that future look like? What will have achieved together? How will we have evolved, advanced, and actualized great, magnificent ideas together?

I have hope that those in that future will look back, and say, "what a waste of time, resource, energy those before us spent for generations on discrimination, erecting and maintaining needless prejudicial barriers against persons different then ourselves. Look at how we have been able to accelerate advancements and prosperity by freeing ourselves of such non-productive policies and practices." This is the grand challenge for true business leaders.

Appendix III:
Additional Resources

While excellent LGBT+ focused resources are always being created, many lack the time to seek them out and properly assess them for lack of bias and significance in fact. The following are excellent references and many provide additional links and options for further pre-vetted information.

Archives and Collections

James C. Hormel Gay and Lesbian Center
https://sfpl.org/locations/main-library/lgbtqia-center
This research center is focused on documenting gay and lesbian history and culture through preservation of original materials and by making them accessible to all. The center is a part of the San Francisco Public Library.

Lesbian Herstory Archives
http://www.lesbianherstoryarchives.org
Located in New York City, US, and founded in 1973, this is the oldest and largest collection of lesbian archives.

Arts, Literature, and Culture

gltbq: An Encyclopedia of Gay, Lesbian. Bisexual, Transgender, and Queer Culture
www.glbtq.com
This searchable encyclopedia includes content, bibliographies, and additional resource links for all things GLBTQ.

Lambda Literary Foundation
www.lambdalit.org
This organization supports and disseminates works written by and for LGBT+ people.

PopcornQ Movies
www.planetout.com/pno/popcornq
This site offers a searchable list of queer films.

Queer Arts Resource
www.queer-arts.org
QAR is a non-profit organization that offers views and discussions of queer art and culture for public career purposes.

Russian Gay Culture
http://community.middlebury.edu/~moss/RGC.html
This site offers literature, films, and history all tied to LGBT people in Russia.

Women in the Shadows: Lesbian Pulp Fiction Collection
http://scriptorium.lib.duke.edu/women/pulp.html
1950s–1960s lesbian pulp fiction is found on this site, powered by Duke University's Sallie Bingham Center for Women's History.

E-journals and Online Newspapers

Advocate
www.advocate.com
   Perhaps the best known and most award-winning LGBT+ website and magazine.

Blithe House Quarterly
www.blithe.com
   A collection of gay short fiction is easy to browse on this site.

GLQ: Journal of Lesbian and Gay Studies
http://muse.jhu.edu/journals/glq/index.html
   This peer reviewed journal focuses on the LGBT+ perspective.

National Journal of Sexual Orientation Law
www.ibiblio.org/gaylaw
   LGBT legal issues from 1998–present.

Gender Identity and Sexual Orientation

Sexual Orientation: Science, Career, and Policy
http://psychology.ucdavis.edu/rainbow/index.html
   Here, readers can learn about Dr Gregory Herek's work on homophobia/sexual prejudice, hate crimes, and HIV/AIDS stigmatization. It is also available in French.

General Resources

Lesbian.com
http://lesbian.com
   This over 20-year-old international website provides links to information on a variety of lesbian-focused information.

Library Q: The Library Worker's Guide to Lesbian, Gay, Bisexual, and Transgendered Resources
https://library.auraria.edu/databases/lgbt-life-full-text
   This site is a librarian's guide for working with LGBT+ people. It offers guidance and resources developed by and for library professionals.

Parents, Families and Friends of Lesbians and Gays
www.pflag.org
   Also known as PFLAG, this site is the home base of one of the US's most famous advocacy and support groups.

Queer Resources Directory
www.qrd.org/qrd
   This site offers more than 25,000 resources about everything queer and is arranged by subject matter.

QueerTheory.com
www.queertheory.com
   This site focuses on visual and textual resources regarding a variety of queer and gender studies and culture.

radfae.org: A Web Site for Radical Faerie Information
www.radfae.org
   Pulling together Radical Faerie information, this source is geared toward a focus on the spirituality of gay men and their shared beliefs in feminism, prioritizing nature, and how individuals can impact the world.

Stonewall and Beyond
www.columbia.edu/cu/lweb/eresources/exhibitions/sw25
   This is an online permanent edition of a Columbia University Libraries exhibit that was created in 1994, in celebration of the 25th anniversary of the Stonewall Riots.

Stonewall Center at UMass Amherst
www.umass.edu/stonewall
   This over 35-year-old resource center offers video, audio, and textual information, and source materials to combat harassment and discrimination of the LGBT+ community.

TransBiblio: A Bibliography of Print, AV, and Online Resources Pertaining to Transgender Persons and Transgender Issues
www.library.illinois.edu/staff/collections-information/about/statements/descriptions/lgbt_desc
   This transgender-focused site provides resources for and about trans identified people and issues.

History

gayhistory.com
www.gayhistory.com
   This website offers an introduction to gay history from 1700–1973. It is an ongoing project that consistently adds new materials.

GLBT Historical Society
www.glbthistory.org
   This organization collects, preserves, and provides public access to the history of LGBT+ people as individuals and as a community.

Homosexuality in Early Modern Europe
www.uwm.edu/People/jmerrick/hbib.htm
   This is a bibliography on homosexuality in Early Modern Europe, which is organized both by country and by subject matter.

Isle of Lesbos
www.sappho.com/about.html
   This is a women-oriented gathering of historical documentation of the lives and views of women both in general and romantically.

Nazi Persecution of Homosexuals, 1933–1945
www.lgbtbarny.org
   From the United States Holocaust Memorial Museum, this online exhibit focuses on the experiences of gay people during World War II.

People with a History
www.fordham.edu/halsall/pwh
   Offering historical documentation of LGBT+ people, this site offers an inter-national look at LGBT+ history throughout the world and throughout time.

Legal

Lambda Legal Defense and Career Fund
www.lambdalegal.org
   This American organization specializes in celebrating and honoring LGBT+ people and people with HIV/AIDS through career, litigation, and public policy work.

Lesbian/Gay Law Notes
www.lgbtbarny.org
   This journal provides information about ongoing court cases, legislations, and rulings related to LGBT+ people.

Organizations

ACT UP

www.actupny.org

  This non-partisan organization aims to end HIV/AIDS stigma and to end the HIV/AIDS crisis.

Bisexual Resource Center

www.biresource.org

  This is a resource focused on the bisexual experience and the history of bisexuality via essays and books, plus audio, and visual recordings.

Frameline

www.frameline.org

  This organization promotes LGBT+ visibility in the media arts field and hosts the oldest and largest media arts event, called the San Francisco International LGBT Film Festival.

Gay and Lesbian Alliance Against Defamation

www.glaad.org

  Now called GLAAD, this is one of the most well-known organizations intended to promote LGBT+ inclusive representation in the media as a way to combat stereotypes and bigotry.

Gay and Lesbian National Hotline

www.glnh.org

  This non-profit offers free anonymous information, referrals, and peer-to-peer counseling.

Gay, Lesbian and Straight Career Network

www.glsen.org

  GLSEN is a leader in the fight against LGBT+ bias in K–12 schools.

Human Rights Campaign

www.hrc.org

  HRC represents 500,000+ LGBT+ members to fight for their equality.

National Gay and Lesbian Task Force

www.ngltf.org

  This politically progressive organization works for LGBT+ civil rights.

Religion

Affirmation: Gay and Lesbian Mormons
www.affirmation.org
   This group has chapters around the world to support LGBT+ LDS members and their loved ones by way of socialization and career.

Dignity/USA
http://dignityusa.org
   This is the largest and most progressive organization for LGBT+ Catholics.

Acknowledgements

Thank you to the New York Public Library, Loyola University Chicago, the Library of the Business of Career at University of Wisconsin–Madison, and the Rainbow Book List for their contributions to this compilation.

Index

accomplice 7
accountability 4, 8, 133, 157
activists 7
advocates 6–7, 166, 172, 180, 182–183
agender person(s) 27–28, 117
AIDS epidemic 144
Albjerg, Lau Viggo 130–133
allies: advocates vs. 7; aggressive construct 7–8; identifying as 6; improving as 12–13; outing LGBT+ persons and 10–11; personality type of 7–9; qualifications of 6–7; risk as 9; supporting LGBT+ persons 13; traits of 7–9; unintended mistakes of 10–12
anti-bullying 54, 90, 107, 128 *see also* bullying
artwork/informational posters 109, 117, 125
asexual person(s) 21, 25, 117
"assigned female at birth" (AFAB) 28
"assigned male at birth" (AMAB) 28

banking industry 160–163, 168–171
Banyar Reich, Lauren 134–136
Barretta, Bill 137–139
bathrooms 2, 97, 99, 110
battle fatigue 18–19
bias 3–4, 16, 31–32, 53, 136, 172–176
bigotry 18
bisexual person(s) 21–22, 24, 117
brave-space offices 2–3
bullying 4, 8–9, 18, 32, 76–80, 99 *see also* anti-bullying
business rules and policies 4 *see also* employee handbook, policies and procedures

Catholic Church 179, 191
cisgender person(s) 21, 27
civil marriage 182
coming out 36–38
community events 91–93
C-suite leaders 113, 121, 124, 170

deaf and hard of hearing communities 16–17
department heads 125 *see also* C-suite leaders, supervisors
DeShields, Greg 140–141
discrimination: as bad for business 183–184; of bisexual people 24; diversity ending 147; employee safety and 37; of gay men 23; laws 76, 80, 182; as legal 40–41; unintentional 35; *see also* non-discrimination
displays of affection, in workplace 64–69
diversity in the office: corporate policy vs corporate culture 157–158; incorporating 90; knowledge testing scenarios 88–89; leadership guidance 88–89

employee handbook: anti-bullying policies 107; dress-code section 107; harassment policies 107–108; office space decorations 108; restroom policies 107; *see also* policies and procedures
employees: family opposition to inclusion 128; inclusion opposition from 126–127
"enby" 27
estrogen 29

fatigue, battle 18–19
financial services industry 160–163, 168–171
food and beverage *see* hospitality industry
food insecurity 41

gay person(s): definition of 22–23; knowledge testing scenarios 51, 64–69; leadership guidance 53–54, 69; outdated beliefs 53; workplace displays of affection 64–69
gender: as binary 26; definition of 26; guided by society 26
gender expression 21
gender fluid person(s) 27
gender identity: assumptions based on stereotypes 33; bathrooms and 97–99; definition of 21; hormones and 29–30; internalized homophobia 35; knowledge testing scenarios 75, 79; leadership guidance 76, 80; resources 187; sexual orientation vs. 26; types of 27–28
glass cliff 120–121
Gray, Richard 142–147
greysexual person(s) 25
group/partner work 88–90
guest speakers 94–96

Haslam, Alexander 120
health insurance: inclusive policies 72, 105; knowledge testing scenarios 70–71; leadership guidance 72
hiring processes: business email addresses 104; emergency contact forms 105; health insurance paperwork 105; job applications 104; job postings 103; name tags 106, 117; new employee orientation 105; new hire documents 103; promotions 120–121; training materials 119; *see also* employee handbook
Hogshead, Sally 148–151
Homelessness/housing insecure 41
homophobia 35
homosexuality 23
hormones 29–30
hospitality industry 140–141, 143–147, 164–167
human resources industry 154–155

inclusion *see* LGBT+ inclusion
inclusiveness 81–83, 152–153, 166–167
intersectionality 16–17, 109, 176
intimate partner violence 22

Johnson, Kenny 152–153

laws: bigotry in 18; changing 33–34; discrimination 59–62; knowledge testing scenarios 59–62; leadership guidance 63; resources 189
learning disabilities 16
learning materials 112
lesbians 22–23, 117, 187
LGBT+ inclusion: artwork/ informational posters 109, 117, 125; as a behavior 167; opposition to 124–128
LGBT+ people: medical/mental professional organizations and 20; naming of 20; spending power of 149; visibility of 181
locker room bullying 53–54

McNamara, Shelly 154–155
McNaught, Brian 156–159
mentors/mentorships 13, 36, 120, 135, 170, 174
Merritt, Jerrie 160–163
microaggressions 35
minority groups 16–19
misgendering 87
MSM (men who have sex with men) 23 *see also* gay person(s)
Murakami, Gary 164–167

names *see* pronouns
non-discrimination: employee's responsibility for 121; as human right 145; policies 103, 107; *see also* discrimination

office environment: artwork/ informational posters 109, 117, 125; collaborative spaces 111; group/ partner work 88–90; inclusion improvements in 113–115, 157–158; name plates 117; pronouns 117; restrooms 110
opposition to inclusion 124–128

pansexual person(s) 21, 117
Pedroza, Alfredo 168–171
physical disabilities 16
policies and procedures: anti-bullying
    54, 80; bathrooms and 99; inclusive
    53–54; see also employee handbook
PostSecret xix
privilege 14–15, 24, 46–47, 121
promotions, employee 120–121
pronouns: in email signature 118;
    knowledge testing scenarios 86;
    leadership guidance 87; in office
    setting 117–118, 126; preference 31,
    34, 39; supervisor's request for
    117–118; they/them/their, as singular
    39
puberty blockers 29
public relations industry 134–136,
    168–171

religion 126, 177–179, 191
restrooms 2, 97, 99, 110
Ross, Howard 172–176
Ryan, Michelle K. 120

safe space protocol 2–3
safety: brave-spaces 2–3; federal
    protection 2; realistic measures 4
Scott, Josh 177–179
sexual orientations: assumptions based
    on stereotypes 33; bullying and
    77–80; definition of 21; gender

identity vs. 26; internalized
    homophobia 35; knowledge testing
    scenarios 73–75, 77–79; leadership
    guidance 76, 80; resources 187; types
    of 22–24
Shorter, Andrea 180–184
silence equals death 146, 181
social media 135–136
supervisors 30, 31, 125
Sykes, Wanda 16

testosterone 29
they/them/their 39 see also pronouns
training materials 119
transgender person(s): bathrooms and
    2, 97–99, 110; business email
    addresses for 104; categorization of
    28; definition of 21; drag queens/
    kings vs. 31–32; identifying 31;
    knowledge testing scenarios
    46–48, 55, 84–86; leadership
    guidance 50, 57–58, 87; medical
    options for 28; pronouns and 34;
    support for 57; surgeries 30;
    transitioning process 28–29; working
    with 32–33
transphobia 35

Williams Crenshaw, Kimberlé 16
workplace see employee handbook,
    hiring processes, office environment
World AIDS Day 132

Lightning Source UK Ltd.
Milton Keynes UK
UKHW021129110222
398411UK00013B/197